The Lies We Never Tell

Fiona Drechsler

More Books by this Author

The Girl and the Wolf: once upon a time

Once Upon A Girl-series Book 1.
A friends-to-lovers, fairy tale-inspired novel about 16-year-old Ruby falling in love with the wolf that leads the wolf pack hiding out in the woods.

Nikki and Greta: once upon a time

Once Upon A Girl-series Novella 1.
A love story (friends-to-lovers, sapphic) following two characters from book 1 and their story of being separated and finding their way back together.

Fiona Drechsler
Rathenaustr. 56
99085 Erfurt
fiona.drechsler@gmail.com

ISBN: 978-3-910642-04-1

Playlist

To My Younger Self (Britton)
Can I be him (James Author)
Quarter Life Crisis (Taylor Bicket)
Iris (The Goo Goo Dolls)
Devil Doesn't Bargain (Alec Benjamin)
WOW (Zara Larsson, Sabrina Carpenter)
Numb (Linkin Park)
Try (Colbie Caillat)
I'll Be Waiting (Cian Ducrot)
In The Kitchen (Reneé Rapp)
How Do I say Goodbye (Dean Lewis)
8 billion people (Kiran + Nivi)
If I Don't Laugh, I'll Cry (Frawley)
Meet Me At Our Spot (THE ANXIETY, WILLOW, Tyler Cole)
In The Stars (Benson Boone)
Outsider (Rachel Grae)
Hold On (Chord Overstreet)
To Build A Home (The Cinematic Orchestra)
Run and Hide (Sabrina Carpenter)
In A Perfect World (Dean Lewis, Julia Michaels)
anatomy (kenzie)
Car's Outside (James Arthur)
Hurtless (Dean Lewis)
What Was I Made For? (Billie Eilish)
Better Days (Dermot Kennedy)

Nothing changes if nothing changes.
But there are also things you can't change.

To all my beautiful broken people out there... If you have to survive until you can live: please do! There is someone who wants you in their life, and maybe they are too scared to tell you, or they don't know how to, or they don't know you need to hear it. But they still do. And things will get better.

Prologue

I NEVER THOUGHT I'd make it to 18. I was sure I'd be dead before then. And still, here I was. 17 years old. It didn't even occur to me at first. I didn't even realize I had almost outlived my self-set life expectancy. But I did. Only eleven more days to get there. That was something to be happy about, right?

But now I had to go through with all the plans I had half-heartedly made in the past years, months and weeks. Traveling was one of the big ones. Going to college, having my own place. Sometimes these didn't seem enough. That's when Lexi would tell me I needed more specific goals. Plans even.

So I made a list.

And I secretly titled it *Don't kill yourself until you did…*

1. See the Eifel Tower
2. Spend a night at the beach
3. Take a Modern Dance class at London Dance Academy
4. Watch all seasons of 'Friends'
5. Dance in a Musical

When my teachers asked me what I was going to do the summer after graduation and I told them I'd go see Paris, Spain, London and New York, they told me to lower my standards. But I liked my list. Made me excited for the future.

And that's all it was supposed to do.

Chapter 1

Somewhere in the multiverse, I am a mentally stable person. This isn't the one.

FOR NOW, I was still stuck in school, with graduation just a few months away. And I wasn't doing too bad. I also wasn't too great either. The bruises on my left forearm still hadn't disappeared, so I wore an oversized jumper in the middle of June, pulling up the one sleeve where the skin underneath looked normal. I made up for it with shorts that almost disappeared under the jumper's hem. Just a normal girl. Just a fucking normal girl.

I had this habit. Not a good habit. A very bad one. Pushing my nails into my skin somehow seemed to be the only way to make my thoughts quieter. And my thoughts were loud. Crazy and loud. And I couldn't stop them.

That morning, my parents had already left. On mornings like this, I was glad and horrified at the same time that my boyfriend picked me up. Glad because I didn't have to talk to anyone else, horrified because I had to talk to him. Someone who would listen to what I said.

Vic's car was my second favorite place in the world, though between his gym shoes and my dance bag the smell wasn't always the most pleasant.

After throwing my bags in the back seat, I hopped in next to Vic. When I kissed him, I could feel time stopping. It could've gone on for minutes if I wasn't so anxious about being late to school.

"Do you have your essay?" he asked while pulling onto the street.

"Yeah, finished it at like midnight," I replied, yawning loudly. "Can I leave my dance bag in your car today?"

Sometimes his basketball practice took so long that we didn't see each other before I needed to get going. Lately more often than not.

"Sure, I think I can even drop you off at dance today." He slipped me a quick smile before returning his eyes to the road.

"Owww, how can I thank you for that?" I put my hand on his leg and he smiled.

"I'm sure we'll figure something out."

THE FLIRTING HELPED my anxiety. I didn't know how it worked exactly. But it did, and I felt like I should be grateful to have someone like Vic who didn't question my weird moods. Like how I went from not texting back for two days to bubbly and excited about everything within minutes.

School was okay. When there wasn't anything too stressful, it didn't really change my mental state. Like awful tests or presentations. Or teachers who felt like calling on people who didn't raise their hands was a great idea.

This day was uneventful. In retrospect, I should've been thankful for that. If I'd known what would happen later that day, I probably would have been.

Honestly, the most stressful time was lunchbreak, when there were just too many people confined in a small space, and no one there to tell them to shut up. It was so loud! Too loud. I seriously contemplated excusing myself and spending my break in the fourth-floor bathroom, which was so far from here, it was empty during lunch. Don't ask me how I knew that.

It wasn't realistic though. I sat at a table in the middle of the cafeteria (the location alone gave me anxiety), and I would most likely bump into at least one other student when trying to get up, which would quite possibly turn me into a shivering mess.

Most of *my* friends had been talking about tonight's party all week. On the other side, Vic, who had his leg pressed against mine, was talking to his friends about the upcoming basketball game. Both of which did not interest me very much right now.

So, while drinking some coffee and taking occasional bites from my lunch, I texted Lexi. She didn't go to this school but was my best friend, nonetheless. Of course she was coming to the party tonight and before that we would see each other at dance, yet, texting her never got boring. Plus, it calmed my nerves to pretend to be someplace else.

"Earth to Jen. You there?" Ellie shouted from across the table. She was waving her hand as close to my face as possible without dipping her arm into the food in front of her, and I was almost sure she hadn't said my name for the first time. When I lifted my head, the girls around giggled.

Nervously, I tucked at the sleeves of my jumper. "Huh?"

What followed were a series of questions about the party tonight. Not like we went to parties probably every other week! Still, they asked what I was going to wear every time. This time, it was precisely the moment I realized I couldn't wear the short dress I usually would. Because it exposed my arms. And I wouldn't get away with a hoodie twice in one day.

"I have this new crop top," I told Nana's piercing eyes. By the Dance Gods! How could she look so intense when asking about clothes? "It has this insane neckline. I don't think my parents would let me wear it anywhere."

"Good thing they don't check."

"They probably aren't even home tonight," I shrugged. If I just kept talking about unimportant stuff long enough, none of them would get to ask serious questions.

Nana laughed. "Oh, so I guess we'll have to expect you two love birds to leave early." She winked, and the other girls burst out in laughter.

Of the things they knew about Vic's and my relationship, the fact that we haven't had sex that much anymore wasn't one of them. And maybe 'love birds' also wasn't the first thing I would use to describe what was going on between us.

Though, if it gave me a reason to leave the party, I'd take it. It was much more fun to spend the night driving around anyway.

Before Nana could open her mouth again, I cut in. "What about you?"

"About… my sex life or my outfit?"

It wasn't that funny. But I laughed anyway. "Both?" I had meant her outfit but if I could get Nana to talk until next lesson started, I would.

When she started going on and on about the guys she could be screwing tonight, I zoned out. My phone vibrated with a new message from Lexi.

Lexi
Just finished school…

Lexi
You're gonna get ready at
my house tonight?

When Nana wasn't looking – which was basically 80% of the time – I tapped my response into the phone in my lap.

Me
Totally! I'm gonna borrow
your green top!

It took her just about two seconds to answer.

Lexi
Obviously;)

AFTER I THREW my school bag in the back seat of Victor's car, I let myself drop in the passenger seat. And off we went. I loved being there. Mainly because it meant Victor and I were alone. I liked being alone with Vic. The other reason was that driving in a car always made me feel like I was free, like I could go anywhere and do anything without my parents or teachers telling me what to do or what not to do. It was momentous!

And with Vic I never felt like I had to be somebody else than just me. He was one of the few people I could be my true self with. If I had known how the day would end, maybe I wouldn't have gotten into the car with him. But how? How would I have known?

Maybe that's why we make mistakes sometimes. Because we don't know better. Because we think nothing bad is going to happen. Because we think the world – our world – would never just fall apart like this. But it does. And it will.

But we're not at that part yet. First, I had to get to dance class. Victor didn't even pull into a parking space to drop me off. He knew I was already late, and with the quickest kiss and *See you later* I jumped out of his car.

Then I rushed into the changing room. Most of the girls I had class with were already there. Lexi too. Well, Lexi was never late. She also didn't go to school like I did. Like most of us did. She was home schooled. Once she told me she didn't like it very much. But when I complained about all the tests and exams I had to do and the mean teachers I had to listen to, she realized it wasn't that bad. That her teachers being her mom and two other tutors was actually an advantage. Her classmates were her four siblings, and they weren't too bad. Being home schooled also meant that she had a schedule much more flexible than mine. She finished her schoolwork most days within four hours, and then she could practice before getting to the dance studio with a lot of time to spare. Our dance teachers loved her. Why wouldn't they? She was always on time and polite, and she was one of the most talented girls there were.

"Have you heard back from any of the dance programs yet?" Lexi whispered to me as we entered the dance studio. We weren't supposed to talk or 'chatter' as Miss Burke called it, when in Ballet class. It was bad manners, she always said. And she didn't allow bad manners.

Luckily, class hadn't started just yet, even though our teacher didn't look very relaxed. I didn't allow myself more than a whisper. "You know you'd be the first to know."

Since graduation was just around the corner, Lexi and I had applied to a few programs together.

Because dance was not just a hobby. It was life. "Why? Have you?" I asked her. There was a reason she had brought it up, and Lexi's silence only confirmed it. "Wait, have you? Have you?"

She grinned like she just got her favorite protein bar.

Catching Miss Burkes' strict glance, she quickly and quietly replied "Later."

"You're evil," I told her. She was. For baiting me, and then not telling me. But there was no way to ask her now. Miss Burkes was starting class.

After Ballet we had Jazz, and after that Hip Hop. I loved dance so much, it always got me out of my head. On this day though, it wasn't quite as easy to banish all other thoughts from my brain. I was way too focussed on not taking my long-sleeved dance shirt off, because it would have meant people seeing the fresh cuts and bruises. And even though these people were more my family than my blood family would ever be, I didn't trust everyone to handle it well.

WE HADN'T EVEN bothered to change out of your dance clothes, when we left the studio. "There are some snacks in the bag, and we have some chicken at home," Lexi's Mom said when she started the car. Like always, Lex and I had huddled in the back seat.

"Merci maman," Lexi replied and offered me the first Twix bar.

We were already late before we'd even made our first stop. Not unusual. Still hurried to get to the party.

Lexi held the car door wide open as I sprinted out to my house to get my clothes.

We drove to Lexi's house where I showered while she changed. At least that's what I thought she did, but when I came back to her room, she was still wrapped in a towel.

"I hate to put on clothes when I'm still wet," she explained after I shot her a confused look.

"That's usually what towels are for," I countered.

Which was when she threw a pair of socks at me. "I know, but…"

"You don't know what to wear."

"Yeah… well, not everyone can have a designated party outfit." It was the moment her eyes flicked to my exposed forearms. To where the hot water of the shower had stung in my bruises, making them stick out even redder against my pale skin. "Are you okay?"

I didn't lie to Lexi. I would have said something like *Never been better* if I did. But my response of "I'm okay" technically wasn't a lie. When I was with her, I was more than okay.

"You know that if you need to talk, you can talk to me, right?" I did. This wasn't the first time she'd offered. "So, do you need to talk?" Her voice was soft and kind. As if I could break at any moment if she spoke too loudly.

"I know… thanks. But I need the distraction of a nice night out right now."

"Alright… Now tell me what to wear."

"Yes, sir." I saluted mockingly and made my way to her wardrobe. She'd already pulled out some pieces that were now discarded on a pile on the floor but there were so many more clothes still untouched. "Red? You look great in red."

There was this red top she'd worn to her birthday party at the beginning of the year, and it fit her perfectly.

"Sure? Isn't it too much for a party? Too attention-seeking?"

"I think it's perfect," I answered instantly and waited for her to put it on.

While both of us got dressed, and our hair and faces done, I asked her about one of my personal horror topics: the future. Weirdly enough, Lexi was the only one I wanted to talk to about it, while she was also the only one who didn't bug me with it.

"Where do you want to go first after graduation?"

"To whatever dance program I'm doing." That was quick. But also predictable. Lexi knew what she wanted. I, on the other hand, didn't. "Where do you want to go first? London? Paris? New York?"

"Wherever you're going," I answered honestly. There was no place I wanted to go to. There was no place I allowed myself to want to go to. Because not going there after I told myself I could would break me.

"Yeah! You and me forever!" She laughed excitedly. "So, where are *we* going first?"

LEXI TOOK ANOTHER twenty minutes to get ready. Maybe because we found ourselves gossiping about all the things possible to gossip about: Dance teachers and other students, dance shows and actors, school and family. In retrospect it was a miracle it didn't take longer. When we finally followed Lexi's mom's call downstairs, she was already waiting with her car keys in hand.

This also wasn't the car ride that changed my life forever. Lexi and I talked and laughed in the back seat while Lexi's mom very consciously and cautiously drove us to Matthew Anderson's house. We had been at that house a couple times before. Every time there was a party it was either at Matthew's place or Matthew was there.

It was 8:30 when we walked through the front door. I didn't know where Vic was going to be, but we decided to go to the kitchen first to get some drinks anyway. Not necessarily because we wanted to drink as much as most people at this party but to have a cup in our hands in case some half drunken guy wanted to convince us to drink more than we wanted to. Vic wasn't in the kitchen but as we left it both with a plastic cup in our hands, we saw him in the middle of the living room talking to some other guys from the basketball team.

At this time of the night, it wasn't hard to get through all those people. I knew that later there would be at least double as many and it would be a pain to get anywhere. But right now, it only took a couple seconds until I had my hand on Vics arm. He turned around and I kissed him. All was good.

I didn't really recall much after that. It was a party like any other. I hung with the boys for a while, danced with Lexi, and had some drinks. Since Vic made a vow with his best friend to not drink this basketball season, he was driving us home. We dropped Lexi off at her house at about half one and then made our way to my place.

That's when it happened.

Chapter 2

VIC AND I were talking. I don't remember about what. It's all very blurry. But I know that I was there, and he was there, and we were in his car on our way to get home.

There's only one moment I really remember. His eyes weren't glued to the street like they usually were. Instead, he stared right at me. I couldn't make out his expression, and I don't remember what he said.

Suddenly his face turned blank. And then his eyes got really big and he stared at something behind me. But before I could turn around, there was a big… something.

Something that changed everything. Something that made me feel so much pain. So loud and sudden, I didn't even know what had happened when it was already over.

I really didn't remember much. Except the suddenly bright lights in the darkness and the fading smell of alcohol. And Vic. I remembered Vic's face.

Chapter 3

THERE WAS NO pain when I woke up. And the crash seemed like a faraway dream. I felt myself take a deep breath. Then I opened my eyes.

It didn't look very heaven-like. Or hell-like. Or white like in the movies, where they go into the light. What I saw was…

Something pink.

I heard a voice. A kid's voice. And as I was turning my head, I caught a glimpse of a small bed in the corner. Too small for a grown person. But big enough for a child.

My back felt like it should hurt, but it didn't. Moving didn't hurt. Sitting up didn't hurt. Though my body felt tingly. And kind of wrong.

The room I was in looked like a kid's room. Lots of toys, tiny clothes and at least two dozen stuffed animals. At a small table next to the window sat a little girl. She kneeled on the floor, while three tiny chairs were occupied by dolls and a teddy bear. In front of each of them stood a plastic cup and in the middle of the table a tea pot. Pink of course.

“Here’s some tea for you. Do you want sugar with it?” Her soft voice sounded kind. And her words seemed practiced. Had she even noticed I was here?

She was still talking to her toys. Didn’t even glance at me. Could she see me? Was this some hallucination? A dream? If I closed my eyes long enough, would this end? Would I wake up? Would life go on?

I tried. I tried so hard. Maybe I needed to lay back down? Maybe pressing my hands against my face helped? Maybe I was supposed to get into the exact same position I woke up in?

Nothing worked. Any time I opened my eyes again, I saw the beige walls, big teddy bears and a pink rug. And of course the girl.

She was hosting her tea party, not even looking up as I constantly changed my position. Getting up, laying down, turning over.

One of her dolls fell out of her tiny chair, and in an instant the girl was there to pick her back up, straighten her dress and hair and offer a biscuit. Without realising it, I sat up, straightening my spine just like they’d told us to so many times in dance. Stared at this weird scene in front of me.

“What is this?” I heard myself whisper.

There it was. The girl moved ever so slightly to turn to me, before changing her mind. She kept on pretending not to see or hear me, but now I knew. Knew that she was only pretending.

“Where am I? And who are you?” I said louder this time. My eyes were locked on her even though she kept acting like I wasn't there. It was weird to see some four- or five-year-old try so hard to ignore me. Why would she do that?

If I hadn't known better, I would believe I was trapped in someone's room who couldn't see me. But I knew she had heard me before. I knew she was trying so hard not to look in my direction because she *had* seen me before.

I tried getting up, only to find that it was much harder than before. There still wasn't any pain exactly, but my knee felt strange. As if it wasn't working properly. Or made out of play dough. I couldn't find anything to hold onto, so I sat back down. Made a noise that had the girl twitch slightly again. But since I couldn't walk to her and she was still insisting on turning her back to me, there was no way to see how she felt about me being here.

Was she scared? It would explain things. I would be scared if someone just showed up in my bedroom out of nowhere. And without any explanation. Maybe she knew why? Maybe she would talk to me if I was really nice? Maybe there was a reason why I was here?

"Hi," I said much more friendly. "I'm Jen, what's your name?" Nervously I pushed some of the hair out of my face. The girl still didn't turn around or speak to me, but she stood still for a moment. "Can you tell me what I'm doing here? Can you tell me where I am?"

Slowly, as though she wasn't entirely sure whether she should do it or not, the girl turned around. Her eyes quickly found mine, and a mischievous smile appeared on her face. “Hi, I’m Mina. And these are my friends: Bubblegum,” she pointed to the teddy bear, “Rainbow,” a doll with a blue jumpsuit, “and Daisy,” a doll with green hair. “Do you want to have tea with us?” Without waiting for my reply, she turned back to the table and put a biscuit on one of the plates.

“Mina, that’s a nice name. Can you tell me where I am?”

“This is my room,” she said in a chipper voice while wandering around the table, adjusting her toy’s seats. She stopped across from me and smiled. “Come and play with us.”

My first instinct was to get up, but I remembered my knee. “I’m not sure I can. I hurt my knee or something.”

Mina glanced down at my leg. Her brows narrowed. “Sometimes I get hurt, and I think I got hurt really bad, but then it just gets better because it wasn’t bad. My mommy blows on it and then it’s okay. Do you want me to blow on it?”

“Not necessary,” I said quickly, “I’m good.”

When I noticed her rather disappointed look, I tried moving closer to her. This time by crawling. My knee didn’t feel weird this time but maybe it was because the situation itself just felt awkward. When I reached the table, Mina had already put another plate and teacup up for me. So, just like I was supposed to, I sat down on the ground and focussed my attention on the girl who was now putting pretend tea in my cup. “How old are you, Mina?”

“I’m five. I got these for my birthday.” She pointed at the pink tea set.

“That’s really nice!” Did five-year-olds know where they lived? Did five-year-olds realise it was weird when a 17-year-old just randomly appeared in their room? “Can you tell me where I am, Mina?”

Her expression changed. Instead of the wide grin, she looked at me with a pitiful smile. I didn’t know many five-year-olds, but I didn’t think they would look at someone like that. “Oh Jen.” In that moment her voice also sounded much wiser than that of a kid. “You know exactly where you are. You have to start asking the right questions.”

“The right questions? What do you mean?”

My confusion didn’t prompt another pitiful look. Instead, she went back to playing with her dolls. “I can’t tell you that. You have to find out yourself.”

Chapter 4

IT TOOK A long time (maybe hours) until there was no more tea. I didn't know whether I fell asleep or passed out again, but when I woke up, I was still in the girl's room, though not at the table, but in the corner, where I first woke up. What happened?

What. The hell. Happened.

By now it was dark outside, and the room was only lightened by a small nightlight that looked like a blue dragon next to the door. Mina was sleeping in her purple bed, her blanket only covering one leg.

A smile appeared on my face before I could stop it. Somehow, this reminded me of a night three years ago. I was 15 and slept over at Lexi's house after a long day of dancing (jumping, learning choreography, accepting that my feet were not as pretty as the ones of others, etc). We had planned to stay up late and watch stupid romcoms, making fun of every actor with weird haircuts. When I looked over, her left foot was hanging out of the bed, and she was dead asleep.

I SHUT THE door and walked over to Lexi; I had only been to the bathroom for a few moments, and there she was: sleeping. There was no space for me to sit at the edge of the bed, so I hauled myself over her, bouncing before landing in my final spot.

Almost immediately Lexi turned around. "I'm awake," she mumbled.

"You don't look it," I laughed, and put my head on the pillow next to her. "Do you believe in love at first sight?" I asked, more seriously.

Lex was half asleep again but tried hard to stay awake. "I think so. There are some things – like love – that we don't need to think about."

I tried to let my words sound light, even though Lexi probably didn't even think too hard about what I was saying, much less my intonation. "And do you think every person is capable of falling in love at first sight?"

"Capable… I think everyone is capable…" Her words turned into a mumble, and I realised she wouldn't stay awake much longer.

"Lexi?"

"Mhm."

"I think someone's in love with me, and I think I like him too."

SOMETIMES I THOUGHT back to that moment, just because. It was the day when I first told Lexi – or anyone – about Victor. In that moment I had thought she would fall asleep and that would be the end of it. Instead, she opened her eyes again, and looked at me for a long time.

NEITHER OF US said anything. She was just staring at me, while I considered closing my eyes and pretending to sleep talk. Not that it would have helped. We both knew that she was the one talking in her sleep, not me.

"I'm awake," Lexi said, leaving a long silence for me to reply. When I didn't, she softened her gaze. "Now tell me: Who's the lucky one?"

We talked another two hours or so, until neither one of us could keep our eyes open long enough to actually stay awake.

THE UNPROMPTED MEMORY of Lexi and me made me miss the old days. And also just the recent days, even though, as you get older, things go from confusing to complicated. In more than one way.

Mina, who was still sleeping peacefully, wouldn't know any of this for the next few years. Right there, with her eyes closed, her face relaxed and her wavy blonde hair softly laying on her pillow, she looked like an angel. A little angel who hopefully would never get hurt or find out that the world was more cruel than you could handle.

Sometimes I wondered if I had ever thought the world was great. If I had ever just felt happy to be alive or if there'd just always been this small voice inside my head saying things could be better. That I could be better. That if I was this or did that, I could actually enjoy life.

The thought made me sad. But mostly, when I started feeling like this, I'd try and think of something else. Try to pretend I was a normal human being who didn't see the world only in black and grey.

Right now, in this weird little world that didn't feel like mine, it took me longer to shake the thoughts. Was I getting bad again? Was that even possible when I wasn't even in my world? Why did this happen?

I was happy when Mina moved, and I could focus on her. Watch her turn to the other side, yanking her flowery yellow blanket over her body before settling down again.

Chapter 5

I FELL ASLEEP without even noticing. When I woke up, I wondered. Why did sleep come so easy in this world? And why had it been so hard before? Why was I here? And not in my world?

"Mina?" I asked as she was climbing out of bed and toward her tea table.

"Yeah?" She didn't even look at me, but she still smiled. Her focus was on the plates and cups from yesterday's tea party her mum or someone had stacked up and put on a shelve with some other toys.

For a moment I watched her take them over to the table – one cup at a time – before thinking about my question again. "Why am I here?"

She giggled. "What do you think?"

Somehow, she seemed way too relaxed. It bothered me. "I don't know. Do you?"

She had moved on to the plates, and calmly walked from the table to the shelf and back, still not looking up. Would've made more sense if they were made of porcelain. But it was just some kind of plastic.

Well, she was a kid after all.

"I don't know," she said in a way that made clear it was a lie. "What is the last thing you remember?"

"I don't know..." Without even realising it, I had tried not to think about anything in particular. Now, the picture of Victor in his car came to mind. The very last thing I remembered. It was just his face, concerned, very concerned. His lips formed a *Fuck*, then it all went black.

I probably shouldn't tell a five-year-old about that. So, I barely touched on what might've actually happened. Not that I remembered a whole lot. "I was with my boyfriend. I think we had an accident."

"An accident? That sounds bad." Her voice sounded chipper though. As if we were talking about the birds outside her window. "What did you do after that?"

"Nothing," I answered right away. "It's the last thing I remember."

A car crash. I must have died. It was the only logical explanation why everything went black after. And why I woke up in a strange girls' room. Why nothing felt normal, and I had nowhere to go.

I was dead.

Fuck.

Chapter 6

"HOW DID IT happen?" Mina sat down at her table. Her teddy bear and the two dolls were on their little chairs. I wondered if she expected me to sit with her, like the day before, but Mina didn't say anything. She just looked at me with her big blue eyes.

"I don't remember."

"Why not?" This time, she didn't busy herself with giving tea and biscuits to her toys, she just sat there and stared at me. It seemed as if she didn't even blink.

"I don't know." Her pressing expression didn't make this any easier. And neither did my annoyance at myself for not knowing and not remembering and not thinking so. Why didn't I remember? Why didn't I know?

This time, I ignored the awkward feeling in my knee and walked over to sit across from Mina at her table. "I want to know," I told her. "I want to remember."

"Good," she replied with a smile. "So, let the memories in."

"Just like that? Do you think that will help?"

"My mommy always says *It can't hurt to try.*"

I could catch myself before replying. *Well, your mom has probably never been dead before.* "How do I do it?", I asked her instead.

"When I need to remember something," Mina began, "I try and sit as still as possible. I close my eyes and I think back to what I can remember. And the rest just happens."

So I sat there. Got in a comfortable position and shut my eyes. I didn't really want to go back to the crash. It hadn't looked good. And although I couldn't feel anything right now, I doubted it would be a pleasant experience.

But did I really have a choice?

Taking a deep breath in, I put myself back to where I knew I was at some point before this memory must have taken place: The party at Matthew's house.

WHEN LEXI'S MOM dropped us of, it was still light outside. That's why there were no kids on the lawn out front smoking or drinking. The neighbours could have seen.

The wide, dark brown door was closed, but we pushed it open and entered the hallway with a handful of people. One staircase led upstairs, another one downstairs, and a door toward the living area, which we took. It wasn't our first time in this house by far, and even if it were, it would have been easy to just follow the music and the voices to the right place.

As per usual, there was barely anything breakable around. The shelves and tables were empty except from some heavy books, people's purses, and plastic cups. There were a lot more people in here. Although it was still early, most of these kids got here an hour ago to get as drunk as possible before they had to leave again.

Lexi and I made our way to the kitchen without any problems. Nobody stopped us or did something so very stupid we had to watch. So, we went and poured ourselves some drinks, then walked further into the house. The living room was a little darker, but there we found Victor and his friends. In my memory I was happy to see him, but now, knowing that something would happen with him and me in his car, I felt an ache somewhere in my chest.

"Hi," I said, and he let me pull him away for a kiss.

Had this been our last kiss? It couldn't have been! We hadn't left the party for a while.

The boys were always nice, especially when Lexi was around. Maybe because they hoped to get with her. Why wouldn't they? She was more than beautiful with her black curly hair, dark skin and almost black eyes. She had something mysterious about her that most people didn't quite understand. When I had met her, it had bothered me, but now – more than ten years later – it was amusing to watch the boys squirm around her. If only they knew she exclusively dated girls!

One of Vic's teammates, Ben, put his arm around Lexi and whispered something in her ear. She laughed. It worked. The other guys around weren't pleased. They knew Ben was actually into Laurie, but they always suspected something more. Something dirty.

"Hey princess," Lexi yelled over the loud music when she got back to me, "we're going to play pool against the boys later, right?" Matthew had half a casino downstairs, and even though his parents didn't know or approve of it, most of the students at Winchester High School had played or fooled around down there.

I smiled. Back when my hair was very blonde and very long, my parents used to call me princess. Only Lexi stuck with it. "Sure thing," I replied. "But let's make sure they don't cheat," I said loudly.

In an instant the whole group got furious. "We never cheat. You cheat!" All the athletes were very clear about this. They were above cheating. So much so, they wouldn't even in a game of pool.

I couldn't help but laugh out loud. "We don't have to cheat. We'll just use what we have." Lexi giggled. We were thinking the same thing.

A FEW WEEKS earlier, I was at a party just like this one. And because it was like it always had been, Victor was there, and Lexi was there, and everybody else was there, too. It was getting late. I was on my third cup of rum and coke, Lexi was deeply in conversation with one of the girls from another school upstairs in the living room, and everyone of Vic's friends had decided to leave the two of us alone for a game of pool. Or whatever they thought we were going to do.

To be fair, after my second cup I always got a little clingy, and a little flirty. Made some of them uncomfortable. Like right now I was standing way too close to Vic while he made his shot, in hopes of making him nervous. It was a close game, and I was not going to let him win.

Unfortunately, his shot hit two billiard balls and he had just one more to take out. I couldn't let it happen. It wasn't even about winning as much as it was about teasing him. Plus, I knew that when this game ended, he'd probably go back to his friends to assure them that no, he didn't have sex with me on the pool table.

Vic grinned at me, knowing damn well he was about to win. Instead of moving closer, I walked away and took position on the opposite side of the table. "If I were you, I wouldn't dare win now."

His expression told me he wasn't about to let me tell him what to do. I hadn't expected anything less.

Like the athlete he was, Vic put all his effort and concentration in positioning himself and the pole exactly right for the almost save win. I could tell he was expecting me to do something. What he wasn't expecting was a loud "Oops", making him look up, and a quick movement of my hands, lifting my shirt.

It worked. He missed the white ball completely, staring at me in utter confusion.

And right in that moment, the door behind me opened and I heard Lexi's voice. "Well, now I'm really sorry to interrupt you guys." I didn't have to turn around to know she'd stand in the door, her arms crossed, trying really hard not to laugh.

Vic wasn't quite as comfortable as me, his eyes darting between her and me. I simply pulled my shirt down and turned to Lexi. "Nevermind, I'm about to win."

Her eyebrows lifted. "What kind of game are you playing?"

The door was still open, and more people came in to start a game of darts or foosball.

Vic walked around the table, putting an arm around my waist. "The kind where she wins," he replied.

I turned my head toward him. "Right answer," I whispered, and felt him chuckle.

A SUDDEN THUMP brought me back to Minas room. I could feel my face heating up, while trying to make out the source of the sound. If this was some weird in-between-world or my imagination, did this little girl know what I was thinking?

Mina was next to the table, her hands clutching something I couldn't see. She looked up at me with a sweet smile. "Did you find out what happened?" When she lifted her arms, I could see it was a third doll, that she must have dropped on her way to the table.

"No," I said and felt my face turning red. "I got side-tracked."

She slowly nodded. "That happens to me too sometimes. Maybe you can just try again?" There was a short moment of silence, when she didn't move and looked at me as if she wanted to say something else. But instead, she just kept going, putting the doll in a yellow dress on the chair next to the green-haired one.

"Do you think it will help?" I asked her. "Remembering what happened, I mean."

"It can't hurt, right?"

Right.

Chapter 7

I CLOSED MY eyes again. Reminding myself I needed to go back to the last party I ever went to. And to not get distracted.

Deep breath.

"WE DON'T HAVE to cheat. We'll just use what we have." Lexi giggled. I did too.

"It might not be cheating, but that doesn't mean it's fair," Ben teased.

Lexi looked at the guys, and probably thought that only very few of them regularly saw girls' boobs. And even though Vic had seen mine before, they still distracted him very much.

Needless to say, we didn't use our attributes that day. But we also almost didn't win.

After the game, we went back to the living room – or, well, Lexi and I did. Vic had to play another round with his friends. I wasn't mad about it. Lex and I would just talk for a couple minutes.

Or so we thought.

Next thing I knew, Nana and Laurie took us to a corner of the living room, where 8-ish people sat on the floor in a circle around an empty bottle.

"Time for spin the bottle," Nana announced.

"OH NO," I whispered. Not at the party, but in Minas room. When I opened my eyes, she smiled at me. Instead of her pyjamas, she was now wearing blue pants and a green shirt. Someone must have helped her change. Could five-year-olds clothe themselves? And would they without anyone telling them to?

If someone had been in here, did Mina tell them about me?

"What happened?" asked the innocent voice.

"I just remembered something I had forgotten," I told her. I was pretty sure it would be inappropriate to mention the game we were playing that I most definitely had repressed. As much as I wanted to remember what had happened that night, I was scared to find out all the things I shouldn't have done. And spin the bottle was probably one of those things.

"That's good," she said excitedly. "It will help you know everything."

"I don't think it will." This game – as much as I did stupid things when playing it – probably didn't have any effect on the night as it went on. I might have just gotten drunker than I should have, but nothing serious ever really happened.

THE FIRST TIME I ever played, I was about 14 years old. Nana had invited me to the party, and I had clung to her all night. So, when she sat down with some older girls and boys, I joined her.

Of course, I had heard of spin the bottle, seen it in movies and stuff, but I had never played it before. Not really at least. From what I'd seen in the movies, it couldn't be too bad, right? I mean, some of the girls from school had played truth or dare at birthday parties, but never with boys and never ever with alcohol.

The rules were simple. The bottle points at you, you answer a truth or do a dare, and if you don't, you drink. Then it's your turn to spin the bottle.

Somebody had an app on their phone, and some of the dares were very inappropriate. I had only seen most these kids around school and barely ever talked to any of them, now they made out and put their hands in their pants in front of me.

Truth wasn't that much better. Not that I had anything to contribute when it came to sex and stuff like that. At 14, I had kissed three boys, and had never had anyone's hand under my shirt.

(Kind of amazing to think that three years later I would flash my boobs at Vic in this very house, just to win a game.)

What I did *have to tell were stories about dancing with dozens of girls, accidently touching boobs, sharing sweaty costumes, getting changed in narrow spaces or hallways full of people, and costume malfunctions on stage. When they ran out of questions about that or just wanted to see if there were any more interesting things I could talk about, I had to drink quite a lot. And low and behold – I got smashed that night.*

Nowadays, I took pride in being a good drinker, but back then, having never had more than maybe a glass of sparkling wine, it didn't take much. Nana ended up calling my mum for me, who had to pick me up at 11:30pm. I almost puked in her car. But she took it lightly. Saying the hangover I'd get would be punishment enough.

She was right.

Even two days later, on a Monday, at dance, I was feeling sick from the alcohol my body hadn't learned to handle yet. Lexi kept shooting me worried looks, but once it showed I wouldn't throw up, she just made fun of me.

"Jen drank too much this weekend," Lexi told the others in between classes. Apparently, I had texted and/or called her that night. Not that I could remember. "She's turning into a real party animal."

Everyone giggled. Except me. I turned to see if any teachers were close. "Say that any louder and I will have to kill you," I told her. Everybody knew it was frowned upon to drink, especially as an athlete. Especially when you were nowhere near 18. If any of the dance instructors heard, they might just get the worst impression of me and put me in the back of all our dances.

And thankfully, Lexi was the kind of person to stop teasing when you asked her to. Emily wasn't. "How much did you drink? Two beers?"

Emily thought she was better than anyone else because she was almost two years older. Her experiences with alcohol started way earlier and had been way more extensive than anything any of us 14-year-olds had done. But sure, she was better.

Although I still felt a little sick, I was very happy when the next class started. And even happier when I finally felt like a real person again the next day.

Chapter 8

IT WAS LIKE my brain didn't want me to remember what happened that night. Or it couldn't. But whenever I closed my eyes now, there was nothing. Nana says "Time for spin the bottle." We all sit down in the corner with the two couches and the really comfortable black rug, and then nothing.

Maybe Mina was right. Maybe something had happened after that. Something I should remember. Something my brain didn't want me to.

But I didn't have much time to think about that. Because just as I was going to, someone entered the room, which had never happened as long as I had been at Mina's place.

"Hey, sweetie." It was an older woman. Well, older as in, she was probably her mum. "Let's have some lunch, shall we? I made spaghetti."

Mina looked up to her. And then she looked at me and said "Can Jen come? I think she's hungry too."

Her mom turned towards me. And my heart skipped a beat... But gladly, her eyes didn't meet mine, which had me know that she didn't really see me. "Is Jen your new friend?"

"Yes, she got here last night."

"Well, hello Jen, I'm Eliza." She turned back to her daughter and didn't break her smile. "Sure, she can come. Ask her if she likes cheese on her spaghetti."

Mina didn't ask me about spaghetti. Instead, she kept her eyes on her mom. "I think she was in an accident."

Eliza didn't seem to be surprised one bit about this statement. "Oh no, what happened?"

Mina's mom led her out of the bedroom, and down the stairs. It needed the little girl to turn around and tell me "Come on, let's go!" for me to actually follow them. I hadn't expected any of this, much less that she would tell her family about me. But maybe it wasn't such a bad thing. Maybe it meant that I really was here. That this was not just something in my head.

And also I was kind of interested in what Mina would tell her mom about what had happened to me. I mean, I didn't know. And the little girl sometimes acted like she did. But no, she just said "She thinks it was a car accident. She was with her boyfriend. I think she's trying to find out more. Aren't you Jen?"

Reluctantly, I replied "Um, yes. Yes, I'm trying."

"She says she's trying."

"Oh, alright dear. Just do me a favor and skip the talk of accidents during lunch, okay? We can put on your favorite tv show."

"Yay!" Mina replied.

When they entered the kitchen, I stayed back and was forgotten quite quickly. Mina got to watch something on a tablet and her mom sat beside her to eat. It kind of reminded me of my mom when I was younger because instead of having spaghetti with her daughter, she ate a salad. And instead of having lemonade, she drank coffee.

I felt bad for invading their privacy, so I went back upstairs. At some point I could hear Mina tell her mum that I had left. But I didn't pay much attention to that.

I tried again with the remembering. Now that Mina had told her mom about it, I was almost sure she really thought that I was going to find out what had happened to me. And apart from that, I really wanted to know myself. Some car accident didn't come out of nowhere. Or sometimes I guess it did. But why didn't I remember what had happened before?

THAT NIGHT, I couldn't sleep. Maybe because I was in this weird world that wasn't my own. Or whatever this place was. Maybe because all I had as a mattress was a pink rug that Mina had moved to my corner of the room for me. She would have allowed me to share her bed, but that just felt weird.

So, I watched Mina sleep. Peacefully. And maybe, just maybe, if I stayed still like her long enough, I would be able to rest a little too.

But instead, I fell into a half-sleep. And the part of my brain that was missing everything about the life I had and the life I was constantly thinking about turned to the person I was thinking about all the time: Vic.

When Victor and I first got together, we were 15 years old. And we didn't know each other very well.

We were in nineth grade on a field trip. Our group was meant to examine self-portraits of French artists. However, we just made fun of the models and talked about French kissing. This girl I used to be friends with – Amanda – said something about opening the door to the other room and at the same time Vic and I said *Alohomora*.

Vic and I started talking more and more and we discovered that we had a lot in common. Between him playing basketball three times a week and me dancing almost every day, we both knew what it was like to be an athlete, and to do everything for your team. And the sacrifices you had to make.

Lexi called it magical when we started dating. I had never had a boyfriend before. Which wasn't that unusual. Most of the girls I hung out with at school didn't have a boyfriend. And even more at the dance studio. But here I was, 15-year-old Jen. With her boyfriend. And now, two and a half years later, it seemed like just the right decision.

Or didn't it?

Something came back to me. Not a memory, but something like… a feeling?

Victor and I hadn't been great these past few weeks. I mean after two years that was normal, right? But there was something like… something I couldn't quite make out. Like… we had a fight and I couldn't remember.

Was it the thing in the car? The words that I couldn't remember before everything went black? Was it that?

Either way. I had to remember what happened. I couldn't get out of here if I didn't know. What had caused all this? What had happened between Victor and me in that car? What had happened before the accident?

I closed my eyes again, telling myself to concentrate. I had to go back to the party we went to on that same night. Nana said "Time for spin the bottle" and we all sat down in a circle. Somebody got an empty coke bottle and Nana didn't hesitate to spin it.

The first few rounds it pointed at everybody else but Lexi and me. And when the bottle's tip finally faced me, I was deep in conversation with Lexi.

Ellie laughed. "Jen, it's your turn. Truth or dare?"

All eyes were on me, and I wished I had listened to what everybody had picked to know what mood they were in today. But I hadn't, so, as always, I just picked truth.

"Tell us about your first time."

Everybody stared at me. Unlike two years ago, now they knew I had a boyfriend, and that we were… doing it. Usually, I knew how to handle it, but this caught me a little off guard.

And because I've played this quite a few times, I also knew that Victor wasn't too keen on me telling everybody what we were doing. Because no matter how I phrased it, they knew it was Vic. I had never slept with anyone else.

So, when I pushed some hair out of my face and looked around the circle of girls who already knew so much and the people whose names I barely remembered, I also debated in my head whether to answer or drink. Lexi lightly bumped my shoulder. "Come on, answer." The rest of it was a whisper. "Otherwise, you will be way too drunk, way too soon." Both of us laughed. She was right.

"Fine," I said, looking into expectant faces. "There once was a girl who didn't quite know how to show a guy she liked that she wanted to do more than just sit on his bed and make out a little. The boy already knew that. He just was too much of a gentleman to show it. So, when his mom and dad were at work, and the girl and the boy were home from school, he led her to his room, and they started making out.

The girl didn't know what to say or how to show that she wanted him to take her top off. Maybe it would seem slutty. And she didn't want him to think that she was slutty. But they had been dating for a while, and she felt ready. And he was the right guy to do it with.

So, when they took a break to breathe for once, she pulled her hair out of her ponytail, looked into his eyes and said. 'I've been thinking…' Like the girls in the movies, she did that little lip-bite-thingy that made him go crazy, but she didn't know that yet. 'When are your parents coming back home? Because… you know… I don't have to get home until 9. And I thought we could try something new.'

He looked at her – speechless. Then he cleared his throat and asked 'What did you have in mind?'

The girl smiled at him. 'Something we might need condoms for.'

And the rest is history."

The next time it was my turn, I picked dare. And the time after that, and the time after that. Not because truth was too much for me. But because I was considering what they might ask next and whether Vic would be okay to know I told them. So, no more truth for me.

The first dare was easy. Almost too easy. Switch tops with someone of your choice. Of course, I chose Lexi. It wasn't like we hadn't done it before. Maybe not in front of quite so many gawking eyes, but as dancers we would regularly get changed in a room full of people. Nobody said anything about switching back, so we did that when it was the next person's turn.

For the second one I drank. No way I'd pretend giving someone a handjob!. Even if it meant emptying the cup. Maybe a mistake after I skipped most of my dinner to get ready for the party on time, but whatever. I didn't plan on drinking again.

I was just about to quit the game – some of the dares got crueller than I liked – when the bottle picked me again. And by some miracle all I had to do was kiss Lexi.

Leaning toward her, I quietly asked "Is this okay for you?" 'This' as in kissing me in front of half my school.

We had kissed before. For fun. For practice. Sometimes to get boys to leave us alone. But not in front of people who might take it too seriously.

And because it was so loud around, and Lexi was talking exceptionally quiet, I didn't hear everything she said. "Sure" – something, something – *"a long time."*

And thus began a whole lot of craziness.

Chapter 9

EVEN BEFORE OUR lips touched, I heard a loud "Oh" in the room. If my eyes were still open, I could see Lexi's grin. She knew what it was like, everybody being excited about two girls kissing. So instead of seeing it, I just felt it when we were close enough. And it almost made me break out in laughter too.

I hadn't even noticed that her hand was on my knee. When we pulled apart, she quickly removed it. It was then that I saw Victor from across the room, looking at us.

Well, looking at me.

And I felt my heart stopping for beat or two.

Shit.

This was exactly the kind of thing that he misunderstood. That when we were playing games and having fun, it wasn't serious. Well, he always took it seriously.

That's when I quit the game and that's when I should have stopped drinking. However, I didn't. I had let one of the guys fill up my cup again after I finished it the round before and now with that same cup in my hand I was crossing the room. Toward my boyfriend, who was still looking at me.

"Hey," I said. "Are you having fun?" I was going for the non-comital what-do-you-mean-this-party-sucks-act.

He had moved a few steps away from his friends and it was clear to everyone that right in this moment, he wasn't having fun. I mean, there was also the fact that he didn't drink. Maybe it would have made him more relaxed. Or maybe it would have made everything worse.

"It seems like you have fun for the both of us."

It sounded bad. Really bad. But if I let Victor stop me from having fun with my friends every time we were at a party together, then I'd never have fun at all. "Do you want to go to the basement? Beat me at darts, and you can have a kiss." It was supposed to sound flirty and cute. But Vic wasn't having it.

He didn't say that, though. Instead, we just went downstairs. Away from the music and the drinking people. When we got there, there was a couple making out on the pool table. Half-naked. And that's when Vic took my hand and pulled me up the stairs and outside the front door.

"It was just a game," I told him, before he could even start.

"It's always just a game," he replied.

I felt bad because I got it. I had told him time and time again that I wouldn't do it, that I knew it hurt him. But I couldn't stop myself. It was stupid. "I'm done playing for today, okay?"

I put my arms around his neck, and he put his hands on my back. Then I pulled him down towards me and put a soft kiss on his lips. "If you want to leave, we can leave," I whispered.

We didn't leave.

We went back to the party and back to our own friends. He stayed with his basketball buddies, and I went back to Lexi and told her with a very certain look that what I had just done was incredibly dumb. We excused ourselves from the group and went to the kitchen to get new drinks. This time to actually drink them.

When we left the kitchen, a song came on that Lexi and I used to dance to. Being silly and a little drunk as we were, we started doing the choreography we learned four years ago. Honestly, I couldn't quite remember much, but Lexi was always the kind of girl who remembered everything she'd ever done. That's why she was the favorite at dance class.

When we were done, she put her head next to mine. "Bathroom," she yelled over the music. After nodding, I followed her upstairs, to the bathroom fewer people used.

"I want all the tea," she said after she closed the door behind us. It kept most of the music and noise out, so you could have a somewhat decent conversation. "What happened with you and Vic?"

"Yeah... No, I don't think I should tell you that."

She held back a laugh. "Sure, you don't."

I always told Lexi everything. She was my best friend in the whole wide world, and even before I was dating Victor, I would tell her whatever big or small things were going on in my life. We would spend nights at each other's houses and not watch movies so much as just talk. Our parents got so annoyed and cranky because we were just tired all the time. But that was the kind of friends we were. "It's the same old, same old," I told her. "He doesn't really like it when I tell everybody about... personal stuff. It's different with you, of course," I said quickly. "I think he knows that I tell you basically everything and, even if he doesn't, it shouldn't be a problem. But when I tell my school friends, they might tell people who are not supposed to know."

"Yeah, yeah…" She ran her fingers through her hair. "We went over this a thousand times, but I mean, he didn't know that you were talking about him. What he did know about was… the smooching thing."

"Smooching thing?" I asked, laughing. "Is that seriously what you are going to call it?"

"Don't answer a question with a question!" she scolded me. "Seriously," that's when the smile disappeared from her face, "what's up with you two lately? Does it have anything to do with the… bruises on your arms?"

"For the record: It's one arm." As if I needed to proof myself, I showed her the untouched right wrist. And maybe I needed to proof to her and me that I wasn't as bad as she thought I might be.

Before I could stop her, she grabbed my left hand and pulled up the sleeve. "Why do you hurt yourself again, Jen?"

"It's not to hurt myself."

"What is it for then?"

"I don't want to talk about it."

"Why not? I thought we talked about everything."

"Not here." Here, in someone else's house. Where there was no way for me to escape if needed.

"Should I worry about you?"

A knock on the door interrupted us. I was a little happy about it. I hadn't told Lexi everything that's been going on.

For a reason.

Because I didn't want to talk about it. It wasn't the happy stuff. And it didn't make sense. I couldn't tell her why when I didn't even know myself.

"Let's talk about it later," I said, as I pulled her up and opened the door for the girl who was about to throw up. "There are some people who need this room more than we do."

Lexi squeezed my hand, and we walked outside into the backyard, deliberately not back to the group who was still playing spin the bottle. There were actually people dancing on the gras, not like inside where there was barely space to do so. And we joined them.

THIS WAS (MOSTLY) a happy memory. But by the way how Vic had looked at me, I didn't think the evening would end up that way. I wanted to stay in the happy moments.

Maybe this was the reason why I came back to Mina's room, when she just got out of bed. The sun had risen and was sending warm light through the windows.

The little girl didn't even look at me, but straight up left the room. Maybe she had forgotten I was there. But so far, she had never just left without even acknowledging me. Did this mean that she couldn't see me anymore? Worry washed over me. Until she came back about twenty minutes later.

"Just pack *one* toy," I heard Eliza yell from downstairs.

Mina had a small purple backpack in her hand. And she smiled at me as she came in. "I don't really need a toy," she whispered to me. "I wanted to say goodbye. I'm going to kindergarten. Bye bye, Jen."

"Oh," I replied, a little too startled to actually put my thoughts into words. "That's really nice." I didn't know what to say. She was just a kid, and I didn't know anything about her except that she was the only one who could see me right now and who I could talk to. So maybe it was selfish of me to think that she was only there to talk to me. That she didn't have anywhere to be just because she was five years old. "Have fun."

"Bye Jen!"

She put the doll with the blue jumpsuit in her backpack and ran outside. And I sat there in my corner. Tried to remember how long kids went to kindergarten.

When would she be back? How many hours would I be alone in here? How many hours would I be alone *with my thoughts*?

IT HAPPENED. I fell back into that trancelike state. This time not going back to the party, because I really, really didn't want to feel that pain again. That pain the car accident made me feel. Instead, I went back to a couple of weeks ago, when Vic and I were hanging out at his house, doing homework. A normal day. A fucking normal day.

His parents didn't have a problem with me being there. But we were not supposed to be alone in his room, and it was "a beautiful spring day", so we sat outside in the yard. There were a table and a few chairs, and we had all of our textbooks and notebooks in front of us. Music was playing from the house's sound system, and this time I didn't sing along. Vic kept teasing me, joking around and tickling me, and I was trying not to laugh too loud because his mom would come out and ask if we needed anything.

I did like his mom. She was nice. But sometimes it was annoying that she didn't want us to have sex and we weren't even allowed to be in Vic's room when his parents were around. They knew we had sex. They knew and pretended like they didn't. But some days there was a new pack of condoms in Vic's room or his bathroom that he didn't buy. Where would it come from if not from one of them?

"Why do I take history again?" I asked him. There was a quiz the day after, and I wasn't prepared at all. Vic was, like always.

"Because you like me." He grinned, and I loved the way he grinned. It made him look even sexier.

"Like you?" I replied. "Why would I like you?"

He pulled me into a kiss and I let him do it. Moaning when he let go too fast. "It seems like you don't like me," I teased him. "Because if you did. You wouldn't be okay with just a second of a kiss."

He laughed. "Oh whatever. Get back to studying."

"Yes, Sir."

I pretended to write down notes from the book in front of me, but instead I just scribbled the lyrics to a song that was stuck in my head. I didn't even remember which one it was, and maybe that made it worse. Actually, it was just this one line, stuck on repeat in my head.

We can always play by ear,
but that's the deal my dear

It was the early evening, when his mom and dad went out on a date. Vic and I were supposed to leave half an hour later. Instead, we went upstairs to his room. Not purely to make out. It also just so happened that I put all my stuff there whenever I got to Vic's house. Both of us needed to change for the party, so it only made sense to go there together. And, well, us ending up tangled up on his bed wasn't anything anyone could've had foreseen (wink). Never had happened before (wink, wink)!

We ended up being late to the party, but it was all for the right reasons. And it ended up being boring anyways. So, whatever.

I REALLY LIKED thinking back to that day. However, now that I was in Minas' room again, and she had still not gotten home from kindergarten, there was way too much time on my hands to just do nothing.

But I didn't want to go back to the night that got me here. What if the next thing I remembered was actually more painful than what I had already felt? What if there was something I shouldn't know, shouldn't remember? Something that was too much for me to handle? What if it all ended once I remembered?

I closed my eyes again, willing myself to not think back to that party, but to any other day. Anything to make me feel better. Less anxious. Less like a hooribIe person.

It didn't work.

IT WASN'T THE day of the party that I ended up in. But it was Saturday night. Summer last year. July, maybe August. I had been looking forward to this day. Because when Vic had told me he wouldn't have time to hang out that night, Lex and I had planned a sleepover. Just the two of us. One like we had done so many times when we were younger.

Most people asked us why we still bothered when we saw each other every day at dance. Our parents, girls from dance, girls from school…

Maybe they were jealous. Lex was my best friend. There was rarely a point where we needed a break from each other.

Vic had some really important family thing, so I spent the whole day with Lexi, too. We went shopping for dance stuff and other clothes and ended up with full bags and sore shoulders when we arrived at her house. The mere thought of me having to take all those things home by foot was excruciatingly painful, but maybe her mom could drop me off the next day.

She was nice like that. My parents couldn't care less.

They weren't around that weekend either. One more reason why I had invited myself to Lexi's house. Two of her older siblings had already moved out and the other four were still in school with her, which meant they all lived in this huge house with at least ten rooms. Eight bedrooms for when all of them had still lived there. Two living rooms, three bathrooms.

Like Lex, all of them were athletic or artistic and therefore spend much more time with their hobbies instead of school. Which sounded way too good to be true. Lucky people.

Lexi's parents had adopted most of their kids and wanted to give them a life that they'd be happy living. Both her mom and her maman hadn't had an easy childhood. They tried to give their children everything they could. And even though I wasn't part of the family I had always felt welcome in their house.

So, when Lexi and I got there that Saturday afternoon, we were greeted by five smiling faces and some fresh lemonade. We spend some time with Lexi's moms and baked three cakes for the next day. Well, one was for that day so everybody could have a bite when it smelled like cake in the house, and two for Sunday, when they had some event to go to.

When it got dark, Lex and I went upstairs to her room and put on a movie that, again, we weren't going to watch. Her bed was way too comfortable to stay awake anyway. That's why Lexi threw me off of it like twenty times that night. Every time I was close to falling asleep while she was talking, she just pushed me over the edge of the bed.

To be fair, I had told her she could. There was really no other way to keep me awake. Still, at some point I just settled on her floor. And gathered most of the snacks around me so that Lexi, too, sat down beside me, our backs leaning against her bed.

"Tell me something," she asked out of nowhere. "What is it like sleeping with a guy?"

At first, I didn't even take her seriously. We had spent at least the last half hour giggling and making jokes about sex and actors and the people who had never dyed their hair once in their lives (me). But when she didn't say anything else, it dawned on me that she actually wanted to know. So, when I turned to her I could see she was looking at me expectedly. "I don't know. What is it like sleeping with a girl?" I replied.

"Don't answer a question with a question!" she told me. "What is it like? In all the movies," she pointed at the screen, "they only ever show them making out and then laying in bed breathless. Like what does it feel like?"

I looked at her a long time before I could answer. She was the only person in the world that I talked about these things with. That's why it was hard to gather my thoughts and put them into grammatically correct sentences.

When I fell in love with Vic, I told her right that night, and she excitedly gushed about when she had her first crush on a girl to me. There were never any secrets between us. We never judged each other for our decisions or questions.

"It's like…" Thoughts? Grammar? "Well, I don't have a comparison. I don't know what it's like sleeping with girls. But you know with a guy it's… It feels really good. I mean, it feels good after you've done it a few times. The first time doesn't exactly suck, but it also most definitely gets better… For me, it hurt the first couple times. But it was still good. I don't know if that makes sense, but you know… Just that feeling of him inside of you is unlike anything I've ever felt."

"Wow, you sound so straight right now."

"You asked!" A nervous giggle escaped my throat. "Now it's your turn. What's it like sleeping with a girl?"

I didn't even know if Lexi had ever had sex with someone. I knew she had dated a bit in the last few years, but I didn't know about the most recent ones. And just as I was thinking that, she lifted her shoulders. "I don't know. The thing is when you're dating girls… they're very respectful when you tell them your boundaries."

"Oh, come on. Not all men are assholes. The first time I slept with Vic he was very careful, and he asked me like 27 times if I was okay."

"Yeah, but that was with Vic. And wasn't it his first time too?"

"Yep, but that doesn't mean he wouldn't have done it like this now."

"Got it," she backpedaled. "And maybe it's a curse that when you're both insecure or respecting each other that much… that it never actually leads to anything."

"Has there ever been anyone you wanted to be with?"

Lexi had a thing for falling for girls and them falling for her, but never actually making anything out of it. I mean, her excuse was damn good. We were both dancing about twenty hours a week on top of school and everything, so that when it came time for socializing you had to make your choice.

She answered quicker than I thought. "Yeah. Well, I think... In retrospect, I would have liked sleeping with someone, but it never… it was never the right time. Or the right person."

"You'll find your person," I reassured her. And I believed that wholeheartedly. Lexi was so great I was sure she was definitely one of my soulmates. She would find someone and fall in love. And nothing would ever go badly.

I CAME BACK to in Mina's room. Remembering that at the beginning of the year, Lexi had had a girlfriend for about four months. They broke up because they couldn't really spend a lot of time together. Ally did some arts program at a big school, and she spent at least as much time drawing, photographing and editing videos as Lexi spent dancing.

But as Lexi had told me they'd actually gone that far. We had celebrated with a movie night. Full of gay romance movies.

I was still smiling when Mina came into the room. Her hair was a bit messed up and she had a huge smile on her face. I didn't even get to ask her how kindergarten was when she blurted out. “Hey, guess what I did today!”

Chapter 10

MINA TOLD ME about three stories all at once. The way a kid does. "And then Paula took the green dragon. Greta drew the green dragon when it was Vikings week and everybody loved it, because there was a story Mrs. Lovelyn reads to us every day, and It has a green dragon a boy who rides it, and..."

I liked being the one to listen for once. To not have to think about everything that definitely did happen and everything that might have happened to me. That night. Although thinking how I was not thinking about it was technically thinking about it.

It was over way too quickly, when Mina left the room for a late lunch or early dinner or whatever it was. And she didn't come back until two hours later, when I was still sitting in that same corner of the room on her pink rug and debating whether I should go back to the memory of that night, to maybe hopefully take me back to my real life.

Like this morning, she didn't even look at me. Her mom was with her, taking her to bed. I hadn't even realized it gotten dark outside. But apparently five-year-old kids went to bed early. Could have guessed that.

Mina chatted with me a little bit before falling asleep in the middle of a sentence. I probably shouldn't have kept her up that long, but I was scared.

Scared.

Of the thoughts coming back. The memories. The feelings. Everything. And at the same time, I was scared to not see my people. I needed Vic and Lexi. I needed to talk to them, to see them, to feel what it was like being near them.

Close your eyes, Jen. Breathe.

I didn't even have a specific day in mind. I didn't care what day to go back to, I just wanted to be with someone other than a child I didn't really know.

I WAS IN the middle of the party again. Dancing in Matthew Anderson's backyard. Lexi next to me. We were having fun. Why wouldn't we? We were together and we were dancing.

Right there. I wish I could stop time and just stay right there forever. But at some point, others came up to us. 'Others' as in guys. Grabbing us. Pulling us in. And I couldn't even see Lexi anymore. But I figured she was just as uncomfortable as I was.

I was sure I didn't know the guy who was pressing his body against mine. He seemed a few years older than me. Maybe he had already left school. I could clearly smell beer in his breath. I tried to step away from him. I tried to push my hands between us. But he was stronger than me.

"Let me go," I said harshly, when he grabbed my wrists to stop me from pushing him away. "Leave me alone!"

The music was loud. But I was louder. And when he couldn't get me to shut up, he just left. My eyes instinctively looked for Lexi. She was on the far end of the backyard. Some guys had circled her. It took me only a few seconds to get there. To yell at them to leave and pull my friend away.

It looked scary. It was scary. And I was more than happy that none of them actually tried to make us come back. Because neither of us would have been strong enough to fight them, and I knew that none of the people around us had even noticed.

"Thanks," Lexi whispered when we were almost back at the door leading inside the house. I wanted us to have a quiet conversation, but all the bathrooms were occupied. There were even girls lined up in front of them. So, we went downstairs. This time no one was having sex on the pool table. And we could just sit in a corner.

"Crazy," I murmured. "Those guys were just crazy. Why do they think that's okay?"

Lexi didn't meet my eyes. "Let's talk about something different."

"What do you want to talk about?" I asked her, instantly softening my tone. She didn't look very comfortable right now. I didn't know what it was. But those guys had messed her up.

"What do you want to do the rest of the night?" It was such a basic question that at first, I didn't even

know what to answer. "It's almost midnight and I have to be home by one," Lexi explained.

Then I lifted my shoulders. "I don't know. I don't want to go back outside. And I really don't want to play spin the bottle anymore. What do you want to do?"

"How about we sit here and talk for a while? Or do you want to spend time with your boyfriend?" There it was. Lexi's smile…

"Naw, it's fine. He's probably still mad at me."

"Because of the Smooching Thing?"

"Yeah. That and…"

I couldn't finish the sentence. I hadn't told Lexie what had happened a couple days before. That things were falling apart. Because if I admitted that, I might fall apart, too.

She didn't press me to tell her what had happened. But I could see that she wanted to know. I sighed. "Vic and I had a talk. About our futures."

IT HAD BEEN Tuesday night. Vic had gotten home late from practice, and I had just finished Hip Hop for the day. And on my way home, he called me.

"Hey." His voice was soft and warm. "You left your notebook in my car today. Do you want me to drop it off?"

Leaving a notebook, a pen, or a book in the car was our secret code for 'I want to see you tonight.' When we barely had time for each other, when we only saw each other in class, but even then, had to focus on other things, sometimes it felt like we needed more time together. This way, both our parents were okay with it.

So, I told him "Yes, that would be great. Thanks."

I said goodbye to Lexi and Lexi's mom, who dropped me off at my house. And looked back for a second before I put my keys into the front door. They always waited for me to get in before they drove away. So, I waved before turning back around and letting myself in.

It was dark and quiet. I didn't know where my parents were that night. But for a while now, I had come home and hadn't met anyone there. Mostly I didn't mind. Sometimes I was happy about it, like today when I could tell Vic to stay a few more minutes than he otherwise would have. Other nights it really bothered me. When I was hungry and dance hadn't gone well and I just needed someone to talk to about it other than Lexi, who was always great at everything.

Anyway. That night I turned the lights on, put my stuff mindlessly in one corner of the kitchen and went straight for the fridge. There was a little note. Probably since this morning, but I hadn't noticed it then.

We'll be back at 11.

There's some chicken in the freezer.

Don't eat the cookies.

The chocolate chip cookies sitting on the counter looked good. But my mom must have gotten them for her work or friends or whatever. I'd probably never know. And if I took one, she would notice. So, I didn't.

There was some chicken in the freezer, but I opted for the ready meal that my mum only kept there in case I really needed something quickly. Today was one of those days. It would still take 10 minutes in the microwave. So, I allowed myself some ice cream, too. And ate that as an appetizer. I had just finished it when the doorbell rang.

It was Vic. Of course it was. My parents still had an hour before they'd be home.

"Hey, beautiful," he said as he stepped through the door, a random notebook in his hand.

"Yeah, I bet," I answered, pushing my sweaty hair out of my face. I didn't even bother to change after dance class ended, so I still wore my baggy shirt that probably didn't look too great anymore.

The microwave binged and I went into the kitchen. Vic closed the door behind him and followed me.

"Your parents not home?"

"Thankfully." I smiled at him, leaning against the counter and waiting for my food to cool down a bit so I could finally eat. "I think I saw them Sunday, so it's not time to call the police yet."

"Your sense of humor is weird."

That's when he tried to pull me into a kiss. And I would have let him but… "I'm sweaty," I whispered.

"I don't care," he whispered back and put his lips so close to mine I could feel his breath on my face. I kissed him, and I liked it. I really did. Maybe a bit too much. It took a whole lot of my willpower to push him away. "Let's go upstairs. I really need to take a shower. Do you want some chicken pasta?"

I put the ready meal on a plate, grabbed a fork, and went upstairs. I didn't even need to turn around to know he followed me. He got settled on my bed, while I went to the bathroom.

A shower after a long day was the best thing I could imagine but I didn't take much time. Not when my boyfriend was waiting in my room. Not when we were alone for once.

When I came back a few minutes later only a towel wrapped around me, Vic was still sitting there. It seemed like he hadn't moved at all. I dropped on my desk chair. I still needed to eat something.

"So, what's up?" I asked him between two forkfuls. Usually when he took that excuse of 'You left a notebook in my car today' he wanted to talk about something.

"I got accepted at Chestwick University. They want an answer 'til the end of the month."

I stared at him, unable to move the fork to my mouth or back to my plate. Unable to do anything. Of course we had talked about the future, but we hadn't decided on anything, just that we wouldn't stand in each other's way of going to our dream colleges. But now it became kind of real. "That's amazing," I finally blurted out. "Do you want to go there?"

Of course he did. It was a great college. With a great basketball program. It was all he'd ever wanted. And it was really far from everything I wanted.

He didn't answer, though. Just looked at me, while my food got cold.

To be honest, when he had called me and then again when I had seen the note on my fridge that my parents weren't going to be home, I thought we were for sure going to have some sexy time. It had been a while. But the way he looked at me, I wasn't so sure anymore. I had to say something. Because by the looks of it he wasn't going to.

"Well, I think I have to sleep on that information." I pushed the plate away from me. I really wasn't hungry anymore. Instead, I sat down next to Vic on my bed. Only then realizing that I was still only wearing a bath towel. Yet, it wasn't like he hadn't seen me in less.

I put my arms around him. "We'll figure it out," I promised. And his warm hands found their way to my waist when he hugged me back.

"I love you, Jen," he whispered.

"I love you too."

Chapter 11

WAS THAT THE last time I ever said I love you? To Vic? To anyone? Was it all over?

Damn it! I needed to know how to get out of this place! I liked Mina, I really did, but I didn't belong here. I needed to go back to my world. To my life.

I needed to know what had happened to me.

LEXI AND I sat in the basement for a while, talking about anything and everything. It was half an hour later when we decided to go back upstairs. Some girls had come into the room. They were loud and annoying, to put it mildly. And since Lexi had to be home soon anyway, we thought it wouldn't be such a bad idea to join my friends again. I didn't see Vic when we crossed the living room toward the group of people who were still playing spin the bottle.

"Hey, Nana. What's the newest gossip?"

"Hey, Jen. You're going to play again?" She had an almost hopeful look on her face. But I quickly shook my head.

"Nope, the stage is all yours. We'll be leaving soon. Just wanted to see if anything interesting happened while we were gone."

"Laurie is making out with Ben. They even took it outside. And Ellie is quite drunk. Great show."

"I'll pass," I replied. "Who's taking her home?"

"Don't worry about her. She gets drunk every weekend. I'll take care of it."

"You sure? Because Vic and I can probably take her."

"No, we're going to my place anyway. If her parents find out she got drunk, they will ground her for an eternity."

"Alright then."

Nana turned back to play the game. She really liked these kinds of things. So, I turned back to Lexi. I could tell she hadn't been listening. Probably because she couldn't hear anything we said over the loud music. But she was also not looking into the same direction as me. Instead, she stared at something outside. Or rather, someone.

"What is it?" I asked her. And she quickly turned away.

"Nothing." Obviously a lie.

We'd spent half an hour talking, just the two of us, but she couldn't tell me what was wrong with her now? Unacceptable.

"Seriously. What is it?"

Her eyes got sad, and she pulled her hair, the way she did sometimes when she got a harsh critique at dance. "That guy over there," her head nodded toward a group of people just outside the glass doors, "he told me to 'show him a good time'. Asshole."

"Lexi…"

"People are so stupid, why do I even care? It's not like that's the first time someone said something nasty, and still I'm shocked!"

"Weren't you the one who said 'It's okay to feel hurt'? It's not your fault they're idiots and it's not your fault if their words leave a mark." Putting my arms around her, I pulled her into a tight hug.

"I know, but it still sucks."

"Do you want to go home?"

"Yeah."

"Then let's go." My eyes scanned the crowd. "Have you seen Vic?"

And then it was both of us looking for him. "He has to be around here somewhere," I heard her mumbling.

"Maybe he's outside," I considered. In here were way too many people, and suddenly looking at all of them made me a little claustrophobic. A little anxious. Okay, a lot anxious. "Let's look there."

So quick I could barely see it, Lexi put her hand on my arm. "Let's not."

Following her gaze, my eyebrows shot up. "Because of those guys? Come on, they're not worth it." And then I took her hand, squeezed it hard, and pulled her outside. I could see one of the boys nodding into our direction, but I ignored them. And hoped Lexi did the same.

It didn't take us long to find Vic and his friends. Matthew Anderson had a basketball field in his backyard. That's where the boys sometimes played during the day, and now, in the dark, they did too. You could think they hadn't done that all week for about ten hours. But I could clearly see Vic, and Ben, and Elijah, and a couple others whose faces I couldn't make out.

Laurie sat at the side of the field, with a few other girls who cheered the boys on. As Lexi and I approached them, I could clearly hear one of them yell "Go Victor!" And it wasn't the only time. She probably yelled his name more times than I had said it all day. All week even. Was I jealous? No. Vic would never start anything with anyone. Not when he was with me.

But still, there was this little pinch. The way your heart felt when you suddenly realized you could lose something you were sure of.

Lexi noticed me stopping for a second. And she was smart enough to take the lead toward Laurie. By the time we reached her, I was back to being my normal self.

"Hey." She looked at me, and in her eyes I could see that she hadn't been drinking as much as I had.

"Hey. So… how long have they been playing?"

Laurie took a long look at Ben before she turned back to me. "About twenty minutes. They're having so much fun. You couldn't even tell it's almost one o'clock."

"Crap," Lexi let out, looking at her phone. "It really is almost one. I need to get home."

Although her parents were nice about her going to parties, they were kind of strict with curfew. So, I got why Lexi was a bit upset. But I could also see from here that Vic was having fun. And having to pull him out of it made me feel weird.

Laurie didn't notice any of that. She looked at Lexi, then at me and then back at Lexi. "I think I need to go home too. Last time I got home after two my mom almost took away my TV." When she stood up, she also caught Ben's attention. Which made both Lexi and me smile. It was cute seeing the two of them finally admitting their feelings for each other. Even if they had to be a little tipsy to do so.

Unfortunately, just because he came up to Laurie didn't mean the rest of them stopped playing. Which meant I still had to go up there and tell Vic to drive us home.

To give them privacy, I quickly turned away when Laurie and Ben started making out. And told Lexi "I'll get Vic."

"JEN? JEEEEN?!" MINA stared right at me. She had never gotten this close to me before. She sat at the end of my rug – well, actually her rug – and looked… worried.

The anger I felt for her pulling me out of my memories, my life, went away when I looked into those innocent big blue eyes. "What's going on?" I had to blink a few times, and then stretch my arms, before getting up.

"You slept all day. Don't you want to know what I did in kindergarten?"

"I slept all day?!" And all night, I remembered. The last time I had seen Mina was when she went to bed in the evening.

"Yes, I already had dinner. Did you dream anything exciting?" It was cute, how Mina got all excited about something as mundane as dreams, then I remembered that she knew I was still looking for answers on what had happened to me. And that she was five years old.

"I remembered some more things..."

"Oh! That's great!" She moved onto her knees and leaned forward. "Do you know what happened to you now?"

"No."

Disappointment washed over her face.

"But I really want to know what you did in kindergarten today."

Chapter 12

MINA TALKED UNTIL her mom came in to tell her a good night story. Which she interrupted to tell Eliza I woke up but didn't know anything new. Eliza's gaze flickered in my general direction, before turning back to her daughter and the book in her hands.

Listening to her quiet and calming voice, I closed my eyes again. It was kind of cute how Mina had woken me up to tell me about her day, but I was so close to remembering what had happened that night! I couldn't let her stop me again. I needed to know.

THE PARTY. OUTSIDE. The basketball court.

Making my way to the boys playing, I had a thousand thoughts in my head. How was it that right now, when Lexi had to leave, Vic was having fun? Why had we – Vic and I that was – fought so much lately? And why did my heart beat so fast, walking up to the boy I'd been dating for more than two years?

"Hey Vic!" I knew better than to walk into a game. Although Ben had already excused himself, they were still all very much in a competition. (I'd had my fair

share of balls landing in my face as a kid to know better than to walk into an ongoing game.)

He was just a few steps away from me, and when he turned, his friends slowed down too. Until all of them came to a full stop. "Two minutes?" he asked, with such a wide smile on his face, I just couldn't deny him anything. But I had to.

"Lexi has to get home." I tried an apologetic look, although technically he *had to be home as well.*

It took him just a second to pass the ball to Elijah, before walking towards me. However, one of the guys had to comment. "When the wifey calls…"

My heart started beating faster again, and I was glad we had already turned around, walking away from them. I couldn't have kept a straight face otherwise.

I hated being the fun police. And him pointing that out made my blood boil. Vic didn't notice, or if he did, he didn't mention it. "See you!" he yelled toward them, then put his arm around my shoulders. We started walking away, and it should have calmed me down, but it didn't.

Anxiety.

It struck me.

I got worse. Again. And simply realizing it made me even more tense than I already was.

But I didn't say anything. Not to Victor, not to Lexi. The way I knew her, she had already sent a text to her mom letting her know she'd be a little late. But like me sometimes, she was an overthinker. An overworrier.

LIKE AFTER DANCE class, I sat next to Lexi in the backseat. It wasn't far, and the routine of it all made me feel safer. I switched to the front when we dropped her off.

Vic took a little longer than necessary to restart the engine. It seemed like maybe he wanted to say something. But he didn't.

I couldn't take the silence. "You're not mad at me for interrupting your game, are you?" Crap. I was still anxious; I was still insecure. I hated that part of me.

"No. I mean... I feel like we need to talk." He looked at me for just a second. Then turned his eyes back to the street.

"About what?" I was fearing the future-talk again. Or the 'What exactly did you tell your friends in that game?'-talk. But it didn't come. He stayed quiet. For just a little too long.

The streets were empty. It was dark. There weren't any people around. And only a few cars every couple minutes. It was almost peaceful. If it weren't for the undeniable tension in the car.

"I'm not mad at you for interrupting the game," he said. And then his voice sounded very calm. Too calm. "I am mad because everything else wasn't right."

"What do you mean 'wasn't right'?"

Another quick look. Another turn even quicker. "You know I hate when you tell people about us, about our personal stuff, even if it's just a game. And you kissing Lexi… I mean… Everybody was laughing! And not about you, but about me."

I wanted to say something, but he just kept talking.

"And it's not even like that's the only thing. You spend so much time with Lexi, and you and I barely see each other. I think tonight we haven't talked more than five minutes. I don't know how many times I have to tell you that I want to spend more time with you. I mean, isn't it obvious? You're my girlfriend. I want to talk to you and be with you. But at these parties, it's always just Lexi this and Lexi that, and when we're together, you talk about nothing but her. Sometimes it's like I don't even exist anymore."

This time he left a pause for me to answer. To react. But I couldn't say anything. And perhaps that just made it worse.

"Have you even thought about what we talked about on Tuesday? We'll be leaving school soon and you have made no attempt to find a way we can stay together. When I told you about Chestwick University I thought you'd say that we should stay close and that you'd find a college near me, or that I should come find a college near you, because honestly, I would have done that, but you didn't even… you didn't say any of that."

"Well, Lexi is my best friend." I took a deep breath. "And I haven't said anything because it scares me what is going to happen… I don't want us to be apart, but if… if we are meant to be together, we'll find a way."

"We won't find one unless we look for one. That's not how life works, Jen. Things don't just come out of nowhere. You have to work for them."

Suddenly his face was lit up by some lights. And I could see every aspect, every detail of his face. His anger. And his hurt. His clenched jaw and the wrinkles between his eyebrows.

And his desperate eyes.

Then it hit me. Literally. Something hit the car. I didn't even get to turn around to see what was coming. But in that Nanosecond before everything turned black, Vic's eyes focused on something behind me. There was a light. Brighter. And brighter. And his anger turned into something else. Fear.

And then…

Crash.

Chapter 13

THERE WAS PAIN. Only pain. And by this point I already knew I was in Minas room and not in Vic's car. But there was still so much pain.

When I was finally able to open my eyes, the sun was in my face. I shut them tight, unable to move away from the sun. Unable to even turn my head.

Everything hurt.

And nobody was there.

Silence was pressing in my ears. So hard it made me crazy. On edge. Feeling like I could explode at any moment.

With nothing and nobody there to stop it.

Chapter 14

IT WAS HARD to move, but it was harder to imagine Mina finding me like this. I had no idea what time it was, or when Mina would come home. What I did know was that she shouldn't have to see me. Not when I couldn't even explain to myself what I felt, much less to anyone else.

This wasn't the first time I felt like this. Lonely. Defeated.

And it wasn't the first time I had to keep a mask on so nobody would see. So, one specific person wouldn't see.

But this time, I had to flee to not show how dark it had gotten. How bad I had gotten. Again.

Only the luring anxiety of Mina getting home any minute got me to get up. It was quiet in the house, and I had only left Minas room once. Never again after that. Well, of course I hadn't, obviously I was dead.

Dead.

Dead!

I had managed to get to the staircase next to Mina's door. My breath was heavy, not from the movement, but from the thoughts racing and my heart pumping so fast... Could my heart even pump... beat... anymore?

Now that I was dead?

Chapter 15

DENIAL.
ANGER.
BARGAINING.
DEPRESSION.
ACCEPTANCE.

I SPENT THREE days and three nights in Mina's tree house. Huddled up in a fetus position most of the time. I only stretched because I felt like my body should hurt. But it didn't. Because I was dead.

The memories came rushing in. No specific order, no specific theme. Just everything and anything all at once. My first day at dance. The first and last dance class I took with Lexi. My first kiss with Vic. The last basketball game I watched him play. A random day with my parents, when they were still acting like my parents. We went out for ice cream because I got into a summer dance program. I was ten.

A lot of me crying in my bed. A lot of me crying in the bathrooms at school, at dance. A lot of me not being able to breathe, but still trying *so hard*.

Confession: I never thought I would make it to the age of 18. Guess I was right.

I HAD CRIED too much. I cried so much I felt numb. I cried so much I felt the need to talk to someone.

On the fourth day – the sun had not come up yet – I made my way back to Minas room. Down the wooden ladder, through the garden and the back door, up the stairs and onto that rug.

It was still in my corner, waiting for me.

And there I sat, patiently, until Mina woke up.

"You're back!" she shouted with a huge smile on her face. "I knew you were coming back!"

It made me smile too; I couldn't help it. "Can I ask you a question, Mina?" My voice sounded scratchy and weird. For one, I hadn't used it in a few days, and also, I was dead.

"Of course!" The girl got out of bed, took her teddy bear, and sat down across from me. Not so close we could touch, but close enough so she could still sit on the rug and not on the cold floor.

"You know, right?" Sometimes I doubted that she was just in my head. Just my imagination. She wasn't really a five-year-old girl. I could tell her things that went through my head. Even things I would never tell an actual child.

"Know what?"

Doubt crept in. Or maybe it was hope. Hope that I was wrong. Hope that this was some weird dream and the party had been a dream and the accident had been a dream. "That… You know that…" I stuttered.

Why couldn't I get it out? On the off chance this person was actually a child and not just my imagination? On the off chance that I might hurt someone if I didn't keep it to myself?

Mina… laughed. The light sound filled the room and somehow made every muscle in my body freeze. "You really have to learn to ask the right questions, Jen." Her voice sounded so chipper, so happy I couldn't even take her words in for the moment. Was this really something a child would say?

No, I decided. It wasn't. "Am I dead?" I blurted out.

Finally. I could say it. It wasn't a big deal.

The corners of her mouth didn't go down. No, they turned into a comforting smile. "Do you really think you'd be here if you *were* dead?"

"Wait, what?"

It amused her. It amused her that I thought I was dead. So, did it amuse me? If she was all in my head?

"But I was in an accident!" I told her. "I remember now! I was in Vic's car, and there was… there was another car hitting us… Oh my god, is Vic okay?" Involuntarily, I turned around, as if he was standing right behind me. As if he'd been there the whole time and I just didn't see.

"He's okay," Mina assured me. Her voice brought me back. To her face. Her face that didn't show any surprise about what I'd just told her.

"He is?" A weight lifted from my shoulders. However, there was still so much I didn't know. "But… the accident? What does it all mean?"

It was like the more confused and anxious I got, the calmer Mina appeared to be. “Now you’re asking the right questions.”

“I do?”

She nodded. “Keep digging. Your story doesn’t end here.”

Chapter 16

AND AS IF she knew that this was the right time, Eliza showed up and got her daughter ready for the day. Mina acted and talked like a kid again. She told her mom about me being back, and how she believed I could make it.

Something inside me prickled when she said that. A warm feeling.

How was it possible that just because this little girl believed in me, I felt so much better? How was it possible that I didn't know her, didn't know what was real and what was not, and didn't know what was happening next, yet I felt relieved? Almost content? Just because of Mina.

The feeling stayed with me for a while, and I watched Mina and Eliza start their day, listened to them in the kitchen, talking about cereal and kindergarten. I heard other voices too. For the first time, I wondered if more people lived in this house.

How had I not thought about this before? Mina must have had a dad, or grandparents or siblings. It was a big house, there were more rooms, and just because I hadn't seen anyone else yet, didn't mean there weren't more people.

When everybody left the house, all the noises disappeared. Suddenly, it was quiet. So quiet I could hear my own thoughts. And my thoughts were *Keep digging. Your story doesn't end here.*

What would happen if I kept digging? Would I find out what really happened? Was I not dead? Was I okay?

Had the accident just been in my head?

No, I could feel it. I could feel where I had been hurt. I could feel where I had been injured from a car crashing into me. That wobbly feeling I got when I first woke up in Mina's room? Probably from the accident. My knee and my hip and my back. They didn't exactly hurt, but they didn't feel right either.

Granted, my joints weren't the greatest after fourteen years of dancing. But deep inside I had long known there was something else.

So, I wasn't dead. The accident had happened, but I wasn't dead.

Was I in a coma?

Was this the world I dreamed about, and my actual body had been laying in some hospital bed all along?

And if so, how could I get myself to wake up?

Keep digging. Your story doesn't end here.

How did Mina know? How did she know there was more? How did she know I *could* keep going?

And why did I suddenly not believe her anymore?

Well, I wanted to.

But I didn't.

Not fully at least.

I had seen the accident. I had felt the pain. I had witnessed Vic's face change from anger to horror.

His face.

Was he actually okay? And what did that even mean? Was he just not dead? Or was he so well he could keep playing basketball?

Basketball... Dance...

If I was this hurt – my knee, my hip, my back – when would I be able to dance again? Maybe I should use the time I had in this weird dream or imaginary land or whatever it was, to do all the things I couldn't do in life.

"I can dance." It came as a whisper. I hadn't even realized I had started talking to myself, or that I had let myself lay down on my back.

"I have to dance," I continued telling myself. "What would I do if I couldn't?" A second passed by, then two. "Nothing," I answered myself. "I wouldn't do anything. School isn't worth the trouble and there is nothing else I want to do."

A silent tear had found its way down the side of my face and disappeared in my hair. "There is nothing I want to do but dance."

I wished I could just... put on some music and dance. Well, I couldn't put on music, but I could dance. So this was what I did.

Surprisingly, the first thing that came to mind wasn't Hip Hop, my favorite, but Modern Dance. I rolled off the floor, as if it already belonged to the choreography, a song playing in my head. Something about sunshine and rainbows.

I looked outside. Sunshine. Rainbows.

My movements started out very sudden, *sharp and clean*, as Miss Lopez would say. And as the music in my head softened, so did my angles. 90-degree knees and arms got wider, fingers looser. And suddenly I was in a whole different world. A world between the one I had always lived in and the one where I was dead or in a coma or crazy. The world where there was only music and dance.

It was interrupted by strange voices.

Well, they didn't quite sound like voices, more like someone had left a tv on or something.

There was no way to tell whether I was just imagining them without leaving the room. But leaving the room made my heart race faster than it should. And it made my hands sweatier than I wanted to admit.

Finally, I reached Mina's door. Without setting a foot in the hallway, I looked outside. Nothing.

No people, no bodies, no faces. But still voices.

And it wasn't just one, as I now discovered. There were at least two. Deep voices. But not threatening.

Actually, they were laughing.

And it made me a lot more intrigued. Who was that? And why were they only here now?

"Hello?" I stammered. No high hopes. Nobody but Mina could hear me. Why would this be any different?

It was quiet again. Was I going crazy?

Maybe I could step outside the room. Just for a minute…

My heart was beating so loud, I almost couldn't hear the whisper. "Someone's here."

A louder, more sarcastic voice replied. "Oh really, Freddie. Why would you think that?"

I heard steps, but I still couldn't see anyone. Until they were right in front of me.

One of the boys was maybe 12 or 13, the other one was my age. Or older. He was wearing a black leather jacket. And caught me staring at it.

"Cool, huh?" he said confidently, pulling on the edge of the zipper. "It's an original Old Punk."

My eyebrows shot up. "Why are you wearing a jacket inside?"

"Why are you so roughed up?" asked the leather jacket guy.

"Don't answer a question with a question," I replied.

A little staring contest, and then the younger one interrupted, and squished himself in front of the other one. "Hi, I'm Freddie. The broody one is Charlie. And you are?"

My eyes darted to him. "Jen." Then I looked back at Charlie. "How can you see me?"

They giggled. "You're dead too, right?" the younger one, Freddie, blurted out.

When my eyes widened, they got quiet. "I am not… I mean, I don't think so… What do you mean, dead too? Are you dead?"

Again, it was Freddie who answered in a very cheerful tone. “Yes! But you...”

Charlie bumped his shoulder to shut him up. “Jen, you said... You’re the girl Toni’s sister talks about all the time.”

“Oh yeah... I just figured you *were* dead, because you stick around,” Freddie explained. “But if you’re not... Why are you here? Did you die... I mean *not die* here?”

“This is crazy. I don’t even know where here is!” Subconsciously, I had backed away from the two guys, toward Mina’s room. And when I entered it, they didn’t follow me. They were gone before I could even wish they were.

What they were saying was insane! They were dead?

Okay, maybe – just maybe – I was scared that they were right... that I was dead, despite Mina saying I was not. And maybe that wasn’t even the worst part. The worst part was that I didn’t know what had happened to everybody else. The people I cared about. The people who were involved. And me. There must have been an ambulance! There must have been another driver! Someone must have called Vic’s parents, my parents, someone to look for us.

And maybe I could remember if I tried.

Chapter 17

ON MY WAY back to my spot in Mina's room I listened hard if I could hear them talking about me. But it was all quiet. Maybe I just imagined it. Maybe they weren't real.

Maybe none of this was real.

The room suddenly darkened. It turned almost pitch black. I laid down on my rug, looking at the ceiling that I almost couldn't see anymore. And then I closed my eyes, letting all the darkness in.

Maybe finding out what really happened was all the more important now that I might not be dead. Now that I might actually have a future.

IT WASN'T THE place I wanted to go. Nor the time. It was way before the accident. Way before my fight with Vic. Way before everything went downhill.

I was in Lexi's bed, drinking Lexi's tea from Lexi's cup. And just as Lexi entered the room, I let out a big yawn.

"Oh no, not again," she sighed, while dropping two bags of chips, some chocolate and ridiculous

amounts of gummi bears on the blanket. "You're not going to fall asleep on me again.*"*

"Leave me alone, I'm heartbroken!" We had just watched the season finale of some show I had already forgotten the name of, and the romantic interest declared their undying love for… drumroll… their ex. "And anyway, it was only once, usually it's you who snores midway through the episode."

"I don't snore!" She let herself fall next to me on the mattress, and threw a pillow at my head.

"Next season!" I demanded. Not like it was our plan all along to watch as much as possible tonight. We never knew when we'd get to watch together again.

Before I even said it, Lexi had her fingers on the remote, selecting the 'next episode' option. She was one of those weird people who didn't have it play automatically. She said it would make her watch all night and she couldn't handle her day on no sleep.

Sometimes I wondered how one person could be this perfect. Discipline, no self-destruction, always a smile on her face.

And how lucky I was to have her as my best friend.

The show began, and almost instantly I turned to Lexi, she turned to me, and we started talking. First about today's dance classes and Emily's stupid comments, then about Christmas (again!) which had just passed, and this girl Lexi met named Ally.

"And she's cute?" I pressed. It was obvious that Lexi wanted to talk about her. But sometimes she was way too shy about these things.

"Gorgeous! And so honest! I don't think I've ever met someone so honest about… everything."

"That's a good thing? I can't imagine being honest all the time, it must get her in trouble a lot."

"I don't think so…" Her gaze wandered to the tv screen and stayed there for a bit. But it didn't seem like she was paying attention to the show. "I mean, just because you're honest, doesn't mean you have to say everything that's on your mind."

"So… really cute, really honest, what else?" Her eyes focused on me again. "What did you do after you met at the mall and fell in love instantly?"

"I didn't fall in love instantly!" Despite her words, she blushed. "We went to that crafts shop, and she told me about her photography. Then we went to JustDanceThings and we talked about dance."

"And then you fell in love," I concluded.

"She's so easy to talk to. It's like we don't even need words to understand each other."

Smiling, I reached for some chocolate. "That's so cute." And inevitably, I thought about Vic and me. How it was the same when we first got together. And how he was still the person I could talk to the best. Except from Lexi maybe.

THE ME THAT was in Mina's room felt a sharp pinch in my chest, thinking about being so close to and so happy with Vic. He had obviously changed his mind. The things he told me in his car that night… it seemed like he didn't feel the same way about me anymore.

"WHEN WILL YOU see Ally again?" I asked Lexi a few minutes later. Although our eyes were pinned on the tv, we still didn't really follow the storyline. The chips were way louder than the dialogue anyway.

"I don't know yet. With dance starting again and school, we haven't really figured out our schedules yet." She glanced at her phone. "But we text a lot."

"What do you text about?" I tried to look at her screen, but she quickly turned it the opposite way.

"It's private."

I held up my hands in defeat. "Sorry, just making sure she's not creepy. Which you wouldn't be able to see because you're sooo in looove," I teased.

Lexi buried her face in her hands. When she came up again, she was smiling, though more of a desperate smile. "You sound like momma. She actually sat me down to tell me 'Even in same-sex relationships you can get STDs'. Ugh." She laughed and I chimed in.

"Oh god. Does she think Ally is your first girlfriend?"

"No!" Lexi exclaimed quickly. Then, a little shyer, she added "But she might be more serious than the ones before."

I could see it. In her eyes. In her smile. Ally was different. And I knew without having met her. Lexi always fell head over heels for her people, but it was never like this. She never looked so… content.

Chapter 18

THINKING ABOUT LEXI made my heart ache more than I expected. The possibility of never seeing her again felt horrible. Scary. Heartbreaking. When I was in the midst of the memory – feeling like it was five months ago today, her sitting next to me, everything alright – I couldn't bear the thought of having to spend a day without her. And by now I hadn't seen her in almost a week.

My thoughts railed back to Vic's words. He looked right at me that night and said I spent too much time with Lexi. Maybe I didn't see it, understand it, because to me it wasn't too much time. To me, it was just the right amount.

And thinking about Vic still hurt.

So, I stayed with Lexi.

Plus, I was still alone, possibly with two dead guys in the next room. I had nothing else to do.

WE WERE DANCING. Final rehearsal before the big competition. The most important competition. To be fair, every other competition was the most important one. If not every single one.

"These skirts are killing me," whispered Talia when we had thirty seconds to get a drink.

I silently agreed while chugging down some water. They were long, blue and absolutely gorgeous. However, they could kill the whole dance if only one person let theirs fan out a little too far.

"C'mon girls, one more time!" yelled Miss Clarisse from the front, and all of us moved back to our starting positions.

One more time was never only one more time. And although we should have finished class forty minutes ago, we still weren't blessed with an end.

We started out in a tight bundle. The first beat was everybody leaning in some direction, the second one reaching, the third one breaking free. And from there on it just became very stretchy, jumpy and all in all extremely exhausting.

While in the beginning my biggest trouble was to not look at Lexi and start giggling, everything after was trying to look at everybody in the most emotional way possible (the piece was very emotional). Including Lexi when we did our partner work.

Of course, she didn't struggle with that. She could grin at me, provoke me, but in the past two years whenever it got serious (competitions, final rehearsals) she was perfect. I told her when we walked out of the changing rooms and toward her mom who was tapping on her phone.

"...and you used to always laugh so loud, I just couldn't stop myself too, and now you're all professional." I bumped my shoulder into hers, and

she bumped right back, laughing as loud as all these years back in dance class.

"Well, some of us grow up." She winked – winked! – and then turned. "Hey maman, have you been waiting long?" They did this three-kisses-on-the-cheek thing. When I was younger, it was Genevieve who taught me that's what they did in France, but to this day I couldn't remember which side to start on.

"Non, only ten minutes." She smiled, got up and turned to the exit.

It was late. Dark outside. Cold in the car. We sat in the backseat, but Lex talked to her maman about dinner, so I zoned out.

When I finally looked at my phone, I had thirteen new messages. Some from Nana, some from Vic, and surprisingly two from dad.

Dad
Hope you brought your house key.
Your mom and I will be late.

Dad
See you in the morning.

Dad
Shut the window in the upstairs
bathroom.

Great. Not just that I would have to get myself some food before going to bed, the bathroom would be freezing when I got home. I loved hot showers but hated getting out and being cold.

“Oh, how nice,” Lex commented. Sarcasm. Our specialty. She peeked over my shoulder, reading the texts with me.

“Yeah,” I answered, half ashamed of how my parents talked to me. “As if I didn’t bring my keys since I was ten.”

“Granted, you forgot them a lot back then,” she added, trying to lighten the mood. That was the year I spend many evenings and nights with Lexi’s family. Who were home when she got off dance.

I grinned. “Or did I?” I did. But I also enjoyed being there a lot more than being at home alone.

I still did, but I didn’t want to be a burden. At some point Lexi’s moms had said something along the lines of ‘She shouldn’t stay more nights here than in her own bed’, and I knew they didn’t mean I wasn’t welcome. But I also wasn’t their child to take care of.

Of course, Lexi knew I wasn’t as carefree as I was pretending to be. And her spidey-senses kicked in. “You can stay over if you want,” she half-whispered.

Technically, yes. It was a Friday night and we would both have to get up early tomorrow anyway. But the thing was: I knew she half-whispered because it was the night before a competition weekend and her parents didn’t like her to spend half the night chatting. (Though we’d both probably be asleep before we finished dinner. I knew I’d be.) And with Genevieve already suspiciously glancing at us in the rear mirror, I declined.

"I don't have time to get my stuff in the morning. And I really need to sleep." I threw on my most apologetic look, and Lex smiled.

"Sure, makes sense. I'll see you tomorrow."

The car pulled into my driveway and we half-hugged before I got out and walked to the front door. After putting my key in the lock, I turned around again, to see the two of them talking in the still standing car. I hushed inside and saw them driving away before the door fell closed and I stood in the dark for a second.

And then I texted Vic back. The last message was sent three hours ago. In the middle of rehearsal.

Vic
Hey, how's it going?

Vic
Oh yeah, you said it would be tense today…

Vic
Hope it all goes well

And then, sometime later:

Vic
Can I come over tonight?

For a minute I seriously thought about it. Like really thought about it. And I liked the idea of him being there with me.

But then again, it was 10pm by now. I had to get up at 5:15. I was already exhausted. And my parents would be home in two hours the latest. It was not a good night to casually invite your boyfriend over.

So, while drinking a protein shake (I couldn't really get myself to do much more) and stumbling upstairs, I texted:

Me
Sorry, just got home

Me
Really tired

Me
Everything alright?

He didn't reply right away which was probably a good sign. Maybe he went out with his friends when I didn't answer, or he was with his family. Or in the middle of some video game. You know, normal things.

After I took a shower my phone binged, notifying me of a new message and simultaneously reminding me to turn it on silent before going to bed.

It wasn't Vic.

It was Lexi.

Lexi
Go to bed!

Lexi
Also love ya

Vic's messages didn't show up until the next morning. When I was already dressed and packed and went downstairs, I checked my phone.

He'd sent them in the middle of the night, plus a selfie of him and Elijah playing some video game.

Vic
Everything's good. Just wanted to talk

Vic
Good luck today <3

Chapter 19

THINKING ABOUT LEXI made me feel warm. Safe. If it hadn't been for Mina I would have gone right back into a memory of my favorite person, but she looked right at me, and I quickly sat up to face her.

"Hey," I wiped my eyes. "How was your day?"

Ignoring my question, she went straight into asking her own. "What did you see? Do you know what happened now?"

I didn't even bother to reply verbally, I just shook my head. Her expression already told me how disappointed she was.

"But… you have to! How else will you…?" She caught herself before finishing her sentence. But it intrigued me.

"How else will I what?" Even though my interrogative look probably wasn't the most intimidating, it was enough for a five-year-old. She firmly pressed her lips together and avoided looking me in the eyes. "Come on, you can tell me! Can I go back when I find out? Can I …" I didn't know what else to want. That's all that came to mind. Going back. To life.

Another thought crossed my mind. "What if it hurts?" My voice was lower now, almost a whisper. But Mina had heard. "The last thing I remember," I continued when she didn't answer, "is the accident. What if I'm going to feel everything? All that pain… I don't know if I can handle it."

A shy smile appeared on Mina's face. "Sometimes we have to feel pain to know we're alive."

"What if I don't want to?" It came out as a squeal. I didn't know I was feeling this way until I said it. It was like the feelings I felt were not mine anymore. They were someone else's entirely. It always felt like that when I got too anxious. Too far into my own feelings. It was horrible. The worst I ever felt.

Mina coughed. Brought me back. It was like a sign there was still *something*. Something I needed to do.

The girl's voice was friendly but soft. As if she didn't know what to expect from me. Honestly, *I* didn't know what to expect from me. "You *do* want to find out what happened, right?" When I didn't answer, she continued filling the silence. "You kind of have to. It's not like you can stay here forever… I mean, you could, but you'd probably be happier…" She didn't need to finish the sentence. In my life. That's where I was supposed to be.

"You're right," I gave in. It was like letting out a breath I didn't know I was holding.

She *was* right. I needed to find out everything. I needed to know what happened. What happened after that car crashed into Vic's.

Vic.

His name should make me feel so much. Love. Hope. Promise. But it didn't.

Suddenly I felt so much longing. Longing for him. For Lexi. For the life I had.

And for finding answers.

"Before you go!" Mina interrupted. I had already been in the midst of laying down, closing my eyes, remembering. But her voice made me stop.

"Yeah?" I tried giving her a smile. But she deserved so much more. For being there. Helping me. And not giving up.

I could tell the words didn't really want to come out. Her hands were tense, and she seemed to struggle to actually say it out loud. "If you don't come back here, you'll remember me, right?"

Only then did I see the tears in her eyes. "Of course!" I said quickly, a sudden lump in my throat making it hard to get the words out. "How could I ever forget you?" She seemed a little better, but not completely. "I will never forget you," I promised, and that made her smile.

"Okay," she whispered. "Now go and find out what happened to you!"

And with that, she got up and left me alone.

I wanted to make her proud. At first there was only darkness behind my closed eyes. It always started out dark. Then there was light. But this time, it came all of the sudden, a quick rush, Vic's face lit up – anger and concern – and then it was dark again.

The accident, it flashed in my mind. *I was in an accident.*

When I opened my eyes again the light was not as stinging, but colder with a bluish undertone. It took me a few seconds to realize I was staring at the white ceiling in a strange room, laying down. And when I turned my head I saw a white door, white walls and a greyish closet. It didn't help me as to where I was. The other side was much more eye-opening.

A window with closed shades, a small empty bed and Vic on a grey chair. Sleeping.

When I tried to shift my weight to look at him, a little growl escaped me. Pain was shooting through my right side, and I sunk back onto the mattress, pressing my eyes together.

Damn! How could it feel so bad?

The sound must have woken Vic up, because he took my hand. "Jen!" His fingers hooked into mine, like they always had. But today my fingers felt cold, and his felt rough, and everything felt a little numb, a little strange.

"What happened? Where am I?" I croaked. I wanted him to tell me it was all okay, that nothing bad had happened. That everything was normal. But I knew it wasn't. And I knew he wouldn't lie to me.

"In the hospital. That car crashed into us."

The memories came back, and I pressed my eyes shut again.

When I opened them back up, he was closer than before. I moved my right hand – the one that wasn't holding his – toward him, ignoring the mild pain shooting through my shoulder, and let my fingers rest on his cheek.

He was here. He was real. I was real.

"You're okay," I whispered. It was a question, even though I didn't say it as one. And Vic understood that.

"I am. Just a little sore." His eyes left mine for a second, and his calm smile turned sad. "I'm sorry."

"No," I replied. "It wasn't your fault."

The door opened. I could hear that, though I couldn't really turn away from Vic, even if I'd wanted to.

But my hand dropped from his face when I heard a voice I didn't know from the end of my bed.

"Good, you're awake." The woman in the green scrubs talked in a soft voice, and her smile was bright. "Do you mind if I check your vitals?" She came around the bed to where Vic was sitting, and he let go of my hand to make space for her.

"What?" It slipped out of my mouth before I had the chance to stop it. Of course, I knew what she had meant. And also that she must be a nurse and checking in was her job. I didn't know what it was I didn't understand.

But as soon as I said it, she stood still. "Oh, I'm sorry. My name is Nadine. You're in St James hospital, and…" She took a quick look at Vic. "Your boyfriend told you what happened, right?" Her voice was even softer, though I wondered how that was possible. She seemed like the nicest person in the world.

The lump in my throat stopped me from speaking, so I nodded.

"Good." She smiled a pity-smile. "I take your vitals to make sure we have nothing to worry about. When I'm done, I will have a doctor come in to explain... your injuries. Is that okay?"

She waited for me to nod again, before testing my blood pressure and breathing. It was over before I really knew it.

"Now, it is the middle of the night," she said calmly. "About 4:30am, so don't worry if it seems a little quiet right now. The doctor on duty will be with you shortly."

I felt like she could see how tired I suddenly was. Her smile was still there. It was something I could concentrate on. "You can rest. If you're asleep, he will come back later."

"Thanks," I replied before she left the room. And Vic was right back by my side.

"I know you won't like this," he began, and his face looked like he didn't like it either, "but when we came in, they asked who to call, so I called my parents... and yours."

It took me a second to hear what he said. "You called my parents?"

"Left a message."

"Makes more sense." Mom turned her phone off during the night. It was her time, she said. Weekdays ten to seven and weekends ten to ten.

"You're taking this better than I thought." His grin made my heart melt. He knew I didn't want my parents to be involved. Because they didn't want to be involved.

"I can text her before she sees the call."

His smile disappeared. "This is an emergency."

"Not really, I'm still alive." As soon as I said it, I knew it was the most inappropriate thing to say in this situation. So, I backpedaled. "They're out of town. Won't be back 'til Sunday."

"You should still tell your parents you were in an accident."

I winced. He was right. And I would have to, at least eventually. But not until they were back. I would not be the reason they had to cut their holiday-weekend short. Not when they'd told me time and time again parties were overrated and young people driving irresponsible.

"So, where are your parents?" I changed the subject.

"Got some coffee and food in the cafeteria." His hand ran through his hair, and I could suddenly see how tired he was. Yeah, while I was asleep or unconscious or whatever, he must have been awake, talking to doctors, his parents, and mine.

My grip around his hand tightened. "You're really okay?" I asked again.

"Yeah, you took the most of it." He looked like he was blaming himself, like he could have changed the outcome of this accident with sheer willpower.

"I'm okay," I whispered.

"You can barely move."

As if to prove him wrong (because that actually was my sole intention) I sat up. My hip screamed in pain, but I managed to not make a sound. "See, I'm good."

My face must've shown what a liar I was, because he looked pitiful again. "You don't have to play the hero all the time. It's okay to be hurt."

"Not if you think it's your fault." *Too much*, I realized. "And anyway, I can't sleep on my back."

It came out as a yawn, and before I could hear his reply, I was out again.

Chapter 20

WHEN I WOKE up, I was still in that same hospital room, but now the sun was shining through the windows, and there were a bunch of people standing around.

A tall man in a white doctor's coat, Nadine, Vic and Vic's parents. Vic didn't sit in the chair anymore, he was in a corner next to a small table with his mom, in quiet conversation, while his dad stood next to the doctor and the nurse, probably talking about me.

Nadine was the first to see I had woken up. "Good morning, Jen. An early bird I see." The same warm smile as the night before greeted me.

Everyone was just staring at me for a second, like they couldn't believe I had dared to wake up *now*. The doctor took the word. "Jenna, how are you feeling?"

"Good," I said, sitting up. It was an instinct. I didn't even stop to feel inside for an honest answer anymore.

"Do you remember what happened?" he asked further.

"Yeah." I could barely hold the flashes back. Vic's face. The light. The pain.

"Well, you were quite lucky. The other driver did not hit your side of the car directly, but rather the front of the car, so your injuries could be much worse."

I felt the silence in the room, whenever this man took a break in his monologue. And I could feel everyone staring, although I forced myself not to look at anyone but the doctor.

"Your right knee has …" It was hard to listen to him. I could only hear keywords. *Overstretched tendons, cuts, bruises* and *definitely healing.*

After he resumed his monologue, I looked at him, waiting for anything else. Nothing. So I took it to mean I could talk now. "When can I dance again?"

There was a somewhat annoyed sigh in the room, and I almost turned to see who it had come from, but I didn't. Whatever. They didn't understand. My parents didn't either. But there was no reason not to ask.

"Well, you should be able to walk."

"You can try it now, if you want," Nadine chimed in.

I stayed where I was. "What about dance?"

"A party might not the best surrounding for you right now." His condescending voice made my jaw clench.

"I'm a professional dancer. I'm at the studio 20 hours a week."

"Well, not anymore."

Chapter 21

VIC'S PARENTS TOOK me home. Or at least they wanted to. Vic insisted on staying with me, so they compromised by taking me to their house until my parents got back. I didn't tell them they would only be back early if it was urgent. And me not being able to walk properly for a couple days didn't quite count as urgent.

Unfortunately, the couch at Vic's house didn't offer the greatest privacy, and his mom didn't allow me to sleep in Vic's bed. Although, as roughed up as we both were, nothing would happen. And Vic decided to rest beside me in the living room anyway.

I asked him to leave while I called my mom. Even though I knew that you could overhear everything being said in the living room from the kitchen. This way, at least, I could pretend like nobody listened to what I was saying.

Two after ten I held my phone in my hand, my moms' number pulled up. It took me 'till 10:04 to actually press the call button.

“Hey mom.” It felt weird calling her. Usually, I only did when I needed something. And that was easy. Question, answer, bye.

“What’s going on?”

“Nothing,” I said without thinking. “I mean… You might have a voice mail on your phone. It’s just…”

“Yeah, I’ve seen that. I haven’t listened to it yet. It was an unknown number. That was you? What is it about? Is something wrong?”

“I’m okay. I’ve been at the hospital last night, nothing too bad.” The words came out way too fast, and though I didn’t want her to ask me to repeat myself, I couldn’t help it. “There was a car accident, and I passed out, but nothing’s broken, I’m okay.”

“Okay.” There was a short silence. Then a somewhat annoyed sigh. “Do we have to come home?”

“No,” I answered quickly. “I can handle it.”

“Okay,” she repeated dryly. “Anything else?”

“No.”

“We’ll see you tomorrow night then.”

“Bye!” She had already hung up. Like usually. At least now Vic knew he could come back in. He took a couple more moments. Maybe to make me feel like I actually had some privacy.

“You okay?” When he finally entered, he looked very concerned. As if calling my family was a whole new accident, causing some whole new bruises. And maybe it was. I certainly felt so much more exhausted right now than just three minutes ago.

"Yeah, okay." He sat down beside me, and all I could do was rest my head against his shoulder. It almost felt like before. My last normal.

When he put his arm around me, I forced myself not to feel weird about it. Given he almost, somewhat, maybe broke up with me just before the accident. Because it felt good. It felt safe.

I should have talked to him straight away. Talk about what had been said in the car before everything happened. Talk about us.

I didn't. And when I opened my mouth to say something… anything, the living room door opened again. His mom was probably worried we would devour each other, when given more than two minutes alone.

"Are you two hungry? I'm about to make breakfast. What do you want? We have bread and eggs, yoghurt and fruit…"

"Yoghurt sounds great," I answered after lifting my head from Vic's shoulder. If I was honest, I didn't feel very hungry right now. That wasn't to say I probably would be in an hour or so.

"Do you need anything else?" Her smile was friendly, but I could see the pity coming through. And just as I was about to decline, she scanned me for a moment. "Some more comfortable clothes maybe?"

I wore the jeans and skin-tight top from the night before, which weren't exactly uncomfortable, but not ideal for resting either. Then again, Vic didn't have a sister, only an older brother, and I worried that Kendra would offer me her own clothes.

"I'm on it," Vic said and got up. Today, making decisions really wasn't my strong suit.

"So, if you need anything else, just tell one of us," Kendra reassured me. "Victor will probably be by your side the whole time anyway." She laughed when I smiled and left the room.

Maybe she wasn't too angry about me being here. Maybe my brain was playing tricks on me again.

It didn't take long until Vic got back, with one of his shirts and some sweatpants. His clothes were baggie on me. But very comfortable. And when he gave me some tape for my knee, I couldn't help but kiss him.

"Thank you," I said smiling. Standing already didn't feel as painful anymore. Or maybe I just got used to the pain. Either way, I was feeling better. And I just then noticed the dark circles under Vic's eyes. My thumbs softly ran over them, my hands holding his face. "You should get some sleep."

"Yeah, you too," he replied as I let my hands wander and rest on his shoulders. "But first some food."

That grin.

That grin made me forget everything else in the world. It was like the earth stopped spinning or the sun shone brighter or the air felt warmer. It was everything.

There were a few moments of us just sitting there. It felt like every memory I had of him smiling like that rushed through my mind in these few seconds. Only to be interrupted by the man himself, turning his head.

"I think I smell bacon. Come on!" He took my hand and almost started pulling, until he remembered – well, both of us, really – that I couldn't walk that fast right now.

I did my best not to limp, but there was not much I could do about it.

Vic was right. The kitchen smelled great. Bacon, eggs, fresh bread and fruit. Everything Kendra had listed was on the table, as well as four table settings. I couldn't remember the last time I ate breakfast at a table and with people.

"Jen, you can sit here," Kendra pointed at the chair closest to the living room door. And closest to the yoghurt.

"Thanks," I heard myself say. Definitely hungry now.

Polite conversation turned into a real chat, and the table cleared surprisingly quickly. Between Vic and his father it wasn't a challenge at all. They were both shoveling food into their mouths as if they hadn't eaten in days.

When Kendra asked if I was still hungry after there was nothing left, I told her no. Breakfast wasn't my biggest meal. I ate a lot at night.

Well, except last night.

"You two get some rest," Vic's dad told him and me and started putting the dishes away. Neither of us questioned it. Getting up was painful because I had forgotten about my injuries again, although sitting wasn't comfortable either. The pain in my hip never really went away, instead, it got worse when I changed my position.

Vic and I laid down on the couch. Even though it was big – one that went in the corner and where two people could lay down easily – we cuddled together on one side, his arm around me, my head on his chest.

I could hear his heart beating, and our combined body heats made me sweat. But today I didn't mind. It was a thousand times better than being at home, alone.

My dreams were wild, but I didn't remember any of them when I woke up. Vic was sleeping peacefully beside me. I glanced at my phone to check the time; it had been almost four hours since we had gotten back from the hospital. I should probably still be sleeping, and I could, I was definitely tired, but it was getting way too hot and I saw a message that I wanted to answer. Well, actually it was more than one message.

Lexi
Did you get home okay?

Lexi
And please no details!

Lexi
Okay, maybe a few details

Lexi
But nothing dirty!

Lexi
Jen?

Lexi
JEN???

Lexi
If you fell asleep before answering, I'll kill you

Lexi
I stayed up just for you!

Lexi
If you have sex right now, I'll kill you even harder

Lexi
But please don't tell me if you do!

Lexi
Okay, gonna go to bed now, hope you don't get an std

Lexi
Okay, that was mean, sorry

Lexi
Nighty!

Lexi
Good morning!

Lexi
Alright, now I'm worried

Lexi
Can you please tell me you're okay?!

I needed to text her right away. Everything else would have been cruel.

Me
I'm okay

Me
Just had a car crash into
me last night:(

The reply was instant.

Lexi
If that's supposed to be a joke
I don't get it

Me
It's not…

Before hitting send I wondered if this was the right way to tell her. I couldn't think of something better, so I just left it at that.

Me
But nothings broken and I can
almost walk normally!

I knew what the next text would say. Knew before it showed up on the display.

Lexi
What about dance?

It hurt me to repeat the doctor's words to her, almost more than it had hurt hearing them.

Me
"Not for a while" and "Depends on how everything's healing"

Lexi
Everything?!

The word stared at me for a while. So long indeed, that Vic turned, almost pushed me off the sofa, and woke himself up as a result. When he noticed I was on the edge of falling down his right arm wrapped itself around my waist and he pulled me closer. "Sorry," he croaked.

It was obvious he had a hard time keeping his eyes open. To my knowledge the only time he slept last night was on the chair next to my hospital bed.

"Go back to sleep," I told him, and snuggled closer. No need to look in his face to check he already was. His breathing was slow and even, and his grip around me loosened.

I kissed where his shirt exposed his collarbone, before getting out my phone again.

Lexi
Everything?!

Me
Hip and knee

Me
I guess I can do some arm choreography

Lexi
Didn't you want to improve popping and locking anyway?

She was right, and you didn't necessarily need your lower half for that. But it still meant I wouldn't be able to train and participate in competitions or apply to anything dance-related right now.

I couldn't let her know of my disappointment though.

Me
You're right

Chapter 22

MY OPTIONS ON how to spend the day were very limited. For one, I fell asleep and was out until about three pm. Also staying on the couch was all I could do. So, Vic and I watched some movies both of us were only moderately interested in.

When night rolled around, his mom lurked in the doorway, probably wanting to kick me out gently. Not a surprise. She'd always been against me staying over. Although these might have been extenuating circumstances.

"Mom, don't," Vic interrupted, before she could even say a word. "Her parents won't be back 'till tomorrow, and she can barely get up the stairs."

"I'm aware, Victor, but this is not your decision to make."

I looked at her for a second, then at Vic, and back at her before opening my mouth. "It's fine. I'll just need someone to drop me off at home."

So, an hour later, after dinner and a box of snacks and lots of reassurance to call if something happened, Vic helped me into my house (although I could've done that myself). That way he could take his time kissing me goodbye and asking me three more times if he should stay over.

I told him no. Not just because his parents would definitely not be pleased, or mine for that matter, but because I needed a little to be on my own.

When he left, the house was too quiet, so I just stood there. One, two, three minutes longer than necessary, hearing their car reverse and leave. The kitchen light was a warm yellow, but everything else felt clean and cold.

I turned the light off when I went upstairs, although the darkness was scary. Not like I was scared of the dark, but if there were monsters to come out right now, I couldn't even defend myself.

Not that I believed in monsters. Not the huge scary, hairy ones anyway. Feelings were much scarier. And more frequent.

Loneliness for example. Was loneliness a feeling? My therapist had had a thing about feelings being a set list. I'd name something I felt, and she'd say "That's not a feeling." But I didn't remember what else she said about it. It was a long time ago.

When I got into my room, I felt a little safer right away. A little more at home. My fairy lights, the familiar bed, dresser, armchair. The paintings on the walls, the yellow shades and the dark blue bedding. There was nothing new, nothing strange, nothing unknown about this room. Nothing I had to worry about.

Yet, when I sat on my bed and looked around, something was missing. Not from the room, but from me. And I felt it as a dull pain in my chest.

I had a feeling Lexi could help. And I had a feeling she'd come if I asked her. So, I had to be careful how I worded things. I needed to know she wasn't in the middle of something important.

Already with her contact pulled up on my phone, I hesitated. Did I want her to see me like this? Not because I was still wearing Vic's clothes, or because I hadn't showered since before the party last night, but because I couldn't move like I normally would. And maybe a little because I smelled of bacon and sweat.

Yes, I decided. Lexi was my safe space. I could let her see every part of me. And she probably wouldn't let me eat all the snacks Kendra packed all on my own, which was a definite plus.

Me

Hey, what are you doing?

Lexi

Tv, stretching, ignoring Mikey

Mikey was her youngest brother. And probably the most annoying one.

Me

You can ignore him at my place?
No one's here and we could
watch that new dance show

Lexi
Sounds good!

This was easier than I'd expected. But then again, Lexi was my best friend, and she always said she preferred my quiet home to her loud one.

An hour later she was there. At 8:47pm we turned on my tv, looking for the show on all the streaming platforms because I had forgotten where it was. And two minutes later it was playing.

Fortunately, Lexi didn't ask me about my injuries. She continued stretching though. On the floor, using my desk chair as an elevation for her over splits. (My desk chair didn't move; I was particular about that when choosing it three years ago. For this sole purpose.)

After one twenty-five-minute episode I excused myself to take a shower. By then, I felt even worse about smelling bad than before. And now, if something went wrong, at least there was someone in the house I could call for support.

Of course, my best friend insisted on pausing the show, and made me promise to yell if I needed her, or text or call. She would keep her phone right next to her.

I clearly had the best friend ever.

When I returned – completely unharmed (at least not more than I already had been) but a lot cleaner – Lexi was watching videos on her tiny phone display.

"You could have watched it on the tv," I told her while limping back to my bed. It was hard to hold the towel I had wrapped around me in place while also balancing on my good leg, so my bad knee wouldn't hurt too much. One should think I was good at balancing since I was a dancer. One would be wrong.

"It's fine," she replied. "It's only been a few minutes."

My pyjamas were folded and under my pillow, so I didn't have to walk far to get dressed. "You can put the show back on now," I told her while yanking my top over my head. "I'm as attentive as I'll ever be."

She did so almost instantly. It felt a little too rushed to be natural. Maybe she hoped it would keep her from looking at me strange. Or from asking questions.

Normally we'd talk the whole time; tonight, we didn't. Only a few words here and there. About the accuracy of the depiction of the dance world. Of classes, competitions and the problems they seemed to face every two seconds.

I could feel how she'd look at me from time to time, as if checking that I was still there. And I chose to ignore it because I knew she must have been worried last night when I didn't answer her texts, and even more worried when I did this morning.

Why did it feel like that night some piece of me died in that car? And how could Lexi feel something I couldn't even put into words?

"You can talk to me, you know?" she said at the same time as I said "You don't need to worry about me."

It had us bursting into laughter. Very needed laughter.

"It's weird," I confided in her. "Last night feels like it's been weeks ago and I don't even really believe it actually happened."

"Why do you think that is?" Her voice was so calm, so safe. I couldn't be mad at her for asking me such a thing, though I would have been if it were anyone else.

"I don't know. Maybe I don't want it to have happened."

"Well, obviously you don't want the accident to have happened."

"No, I mean everything … The party was fun and all, but then things just got out of hand …"

"What do you mean?" She turned fully toward me, even forgetting to stretch. Neither of us were watching the show anymore.

It took me a few moments to answer. Flashbacks of last night played before my eyes. "Vic was really angry. I think he wanted to break up with me, just before it happened."

Even calm and collected Lexi didn't know how to answer that. Her eyes were fixed on the wall behind me, just next to my head.

"Damn," she sighed. "Why?"

I didn't want to say the first thing that came to mind: You. Instead, I dug deeper into what he'd said. "We've kind of been growing apart. I don't know where I'll be after graduation and apparently, he wanted me to tell him not to go to Chestwick University or to find some place where we could be close."

"Isn't that the exact opposite to what you agreed on last year?"

For some reason I chuckled. No idea why. "That's exactly what I thought." I put my towel on the back of my desk chair. "But now I think he might be right. If we don't… Long distance shit doesn't work. And it's not like we're unhappy together, so why not take a chance?"

"Because you deserve better than *not unhappy together.*"

Chapter 23

SHE HAD A point. And I kept thinking about it long after we turned the tv off and laid down in bed. Lex was already breathing evenly next to me, and I didn't dare to move. But the thoughts raced through my head.

I did want more than *not unhappy.* And maybe it was because Vic and I were out of the honeymoon phase that I didn't use other words. But he could make me happy. More than happy. He could make me smile and laugh and moan. He could make me feel pretty and safe and loved.

But then again, he didn't just talk about our future in the car. There was also a huge part about me spending all my time with Lexi. And maybe he was right. Well, obviously he was right.

It dawned on me that I had done it again. Sent him away and invited her over.

But hadn't I just spent all day with him at his parents' house? To be fair, we hadn't had much time to ourselves and all we did was lay on the couch, but we did spend the day together. And he had been sweet and funny and hadn't even mentioned the breakup-speech.

Possibly because breaking up with someone you had just been in an accident with was more than bad timing. It was cruel.

Though I didn't like the not-knowing very much either.

My phone lit up with a message from none other than Vic himself. Apparently, he had already sent me a few texts earlier that I forgot to check. For a second I debated whether I should answer them right away. After all, he was my boyfriend, and for all he knew I was alone at my house right now.

It was only fair to reply, right?

Right?

I didn't feel like answering at all. My eyes were tired, and I was afraid I'd wake up Lexi with the light coming from the screen. But once I opened his messages, I couldn't just leave him on read. Now, that would be rude.

The last one read: *I guess you're sleeping. Night!*

Did I have to feel bad about not checking in earlier? Should I have answered him straight away? Keeping the sound on my phone on just so I could reply instantly?

All his other messages weren't very important. Just asking how I was and whether I needed something. If I answered now, he'd know I wasn't asleep. And if I didn't answer until the morning, I would feel like crap.

He was still my boyfriend. I shouldn't be an asshole.

But maybe talking about the same things over and over again made me tired. Maybe today I didn't want to talk about how I was feeling anymore.

THE SUN CREPT through my window in the morning, and I had some trouble opening my eyes. After all, I didn't have to. It was a Sunday, and there was nothing to do except rest.

Next to me Lexi was breathing slowly, obviously still asleep. It felt good having her next to me. Not being alone. Although most days I didn't mind being alone. I kind of enjoyed it from time to time.

Those were the days I spent sleeping in, eating and reading a lot, and possibly putting my future into lists I'd never get to completing.

Not to be confused with the days I hated being alone and hated everything else in the world too. When nothing really mattered anymore and I'd just lay in bed all day, or as long as it took someone to come and check on me. Then I'd pretend I was fine, get up, shower and put on a fake smile.

I never had to fake a smile with Lexi. But I sometimes did around Vic. What did that mean?

My hand pushed something out of my face. A piece of paper stuck to my forehead. I didn't remember any paper in my bed. Weird.

It was tiny. Like someone had ripped up a normal sized piece of paper into small bits to leave miniature notes.

I had to squint my eyes to read the little letters.

You know
I love you, right?

Just as I'd read it, smiled and put it away, I heard something next to me. Of course, Lexi.

When I turned back to her, big brown eyes looked at me, a giant grin on her lips. "You know I love you, right?" she whispered.

"You just say that because I almost died last night."

Her hand pushed my shoulder. "Don't say that." She tucked a strand of hair behind my ear. "You didn't, did you?" she added more seriously. "Almost die?"

"No," I said. "But humour is so much easier than feelings."

"I know." Thankfully, she wanted to talk about death as much as I did. Not. "What are you going to do about Vic?"

"I have no idea."

And I didn't.

And I felt like maybe I wasn't supposed to figure this out right now. Maybe I was just supposed to sleep a little more, and let my injuries heal, before heading into the next big catastrophe.

But of course this wasn't how it happened. I answered his messages as neutral as I could. Saying I would spend the day with Lexi. Although apparently, Vic and I had made plans to go to the cinema that night.

But since I wasn't well on my feet, and I didn't really want to walk all the way downtown, that wasn't going to happen anyway. So, I had a few more hours, days maybe, to make a decision.

Lexi and I didn't do much either, though I let her talk me into leaving the .house... into shopping of all things. It wasn't great walking around, but the doctor had told me to walk whenever I didn't feel too much pain, so my muscles could get back to the usual workload. Especially if I wanted to go back into dancing as soon as possible. Which I did.

We shopped at the dance outlet we always went to, and looked at the same t-shirts they already had in store the last time we were there.

My mom usually didn't text me when they were about to get back from their weekend get-aways, but this time she did. Maybe because of the accident. Or maybe because she remembered it was almost my birthday and she hadn't talked to me for almost a week before last night.

And even worse than that, mom and dad got home pretty early that night and wanted to take me out to dinner.

"Um... okay," I stuttered. I was wearing sweatpants and a baggie shirt that I'd been wearing all day. My knee support didn't fit under any of my jeans. Mom had noticed and the look on her face spoke volumes. I was definitely not allowed to go out like this. With them at least.

Well, I knew her and dad too well to even assume they would let me go to dinner dressed sloppy, so I put on a nice dress, and pulled the knee support over my tights. It was kind of ugly, but the colour somehow fit with the dress.

When we sat in the restaurant, we looked like a perfect family. Though, the picture would probably be the same with any other child. Any other well-dressed, well-behaved child. Didn't have to be me.

The night started as I expected. Nobody was blatantly annoyed, but nobody seemed happy to be there either. When mom read the label of the wine bottle in front of her, the silence got deafening.

People around us were chatting, but our table stayed quiet. And since we were out, I couldn't text anyone about my destiny. Not even under the table.

Instead, I pretended to look around, impressed by the fake silver statues that were incredibly ugly, and intrigued by the light blue colours, the restaurant decided was the best colour-scheme to display.

If I was being honest, it just reminded me of a hospital. And lately I didn't really fancy the ambiance, even if it was glamourized.

"So Jenna, how was your weekend?" was how my dad chose to break the silence. Only to receive a nasty look from my mom.

"Good, except the hospital part, that was kind of annoying." It slipped out before I could stop it. Actually, I had intended to not talk about serious things: hospitals, futures and so on. But now that I did, I had to own it, and put a polite smile on my face, even though it cost so much energy.

Nonetheless, it worked. If I looked close enough, I could almost see an eyeroll from mom. Though she'd never admit it.

"What hospital were you at?" asked mom.

God, what did I do?! "The one in the city. St. James."

"What was the doctor's name?"

"I don't remember… Springsteen or something…"

"And did he treat you well?"

"I guess…"

Thankfully, a waiter appeared, and I didn't get another bunch of questions right then and there. But this little exchange alone didn't help the situation. Not even close. I could have used some carbs right about now.

Unfortunately, dinner with my parents started with salads and soups. And my go-to salad didn't have any carbs. Not much of anything, if we were being honest. Not even much protein, with only a few leaves, carrots and cucumber. Thank the Dance Gods this wasn't all of my dinner!

And thank the Dance Gods we didn't speak while eating!

When I was younger, going out to eat was an adventure. We would pick a random restaurant, order whatever sounded good, and took bites of each other's meals to determine the best. We'd skip appetizers but have desserts whenever we wanted some and went to the movies after.

All we'd be doing after tonight was sit in a quiet car together, go home and pretend we'd spend enough time with each other, so we could all go our separate ways.

When the waiter took our plates, there was suddenly enough room to speak again. And I hated it. The first thing dad declared was way too upbeat. "Well, I for one, really enjoyed our weekend, even though the mountains are not my favourite destination. But this really puts a nice end to it, don't you think, darling?" He looked at my mom, and I was glad to be left out of the conversation. If only mom didn't feel like scolding him for saying he'd enjoyed the weekend his daughter got hit by a car.

"How was your trip?" I cut in, before she could bring the conversation back to me. "Did you go hiking?"

"Yes, we did. But only once." My mom's face turned into a grimace, as if she'd really expected to go more than once during a two-day trip. "My legs are sore, I can tell you that. I'm certainly not used to the exercise anymore."

What a lie! She went to the gym three times a week, maybe more. There was one in the building where she worked. But I didn't say anything like that. Just smiled and nodded.

"Oh yes, what a shame!" my dad agreed. Though we all knew he didn't. "But they had a whirlpool and sauna, and those are supposed to be good for sore muscles." I knew what he said less loud and in my mom's ear was something about going to that sauna in the city, even without hearing any of it.

And then the waiter came back. With more plates. I wasn't hungry, but I knew better than to tell my parents. They surely weren't too happy about Lexi staying over and us eating a full-blown breakfast-lunch and then a truck load of snacks and a second lunch at the mall. And I wouldn't even blame them.

Surprisingly, my mom talked to me, while eating. Of course, she had swallowed all her food, put her cutlery aside for a second and looked at me with sudden interest. "How are applications going? Any responses from colleges?"

It had been a sore topic between us, and it dawned on me that this might be the only reason we were out for food. Because at home I could just disappear to my room and pretend I hadn't heard her.

"Not yet," I replied between two bites, although that wasn't true. I'd gotten a few invitations to present my skills in person. But mom wasn't talking about dance programs.

"Not even Chestwick University? Their mathematics program is very good. You always liked math."

"Not enough to study it." I was applying to some IT and computer linguistics programs but didn't have high hopes. For one, I had never done anything in those fields except one or two school projects, and two, all my free time was filled with dance. There was no way I'd actually enjoy spending nights on end coding.

"Not even to stay close to Victor? I thought you two were serious." I hated myself for having told her about it. And even more so, that I had to play it cool right now.

"We are serious, but choosing a college is a very definite decision."

"Is that why you don't make one?"

For a moment I forgot to eat and stared into her eyes instead. "I'm not even sure I want to go to any school straight away."

She sighed. A terribly annoyed sigh. *We've been over this*, it said. *Education is important.*

"Nana will spend the summer in Thailand, building houses. And Elijah will work and travel through Australia, before going to college next year."

Mom was back to putting appropriate amounts of very healthy food in her mouth, and for a couple of minutes we all ate in silence. I dreaded that last bite. It was clear my mom had fundamentally different plans for me, and that deciding against them made her irritated. Irritated mom wasn't nice.

"How about this," she said, when her plate was empty. "You travel this summer, but in the fall, you'll go get an education."

She said it like it was a negotiation, not my future. Fine. Two could play this game. "How about this. I make up my mind on what I'll do, and then I'll let you know."

Needless to say, she didn't like the idea very much. But good for me, she didn't want to start a fight in the middle of the restaurant. "I'm just saying, you don't have much time left for applications."

I left it at that. She tried. Tried not to flip. And I'd rather have her mildly annoyed than full-blown irritated. Went away easier too.

The restaurant only got fuller the later it got, and when we finally left (without dessert, because *who could eat dessert after appetizer and main course?*) there were already people waiting to get our table.

The drive home was as quiet as the one that got us there, and I was happy about that. If nobody ever asked me about my future again, it would still be too soon.

Chapter 24

IT FELT WEIRD getting home after that. For one, my parents hadn't invited me to watch a movie together after dinner in eternities. But there was also this awkward tension, as if they wanted to ask something more. Something they didn't actually want to say out loud.

Picking a film was easy with my parents. It was the only thing speaking for this. However, documentaries never actually interested me that much. Especially if it was about prehistoric water-amphibs or the accidental discovery of porcelain.

Tonight, we opted for *The Magical World of Fairy Tales*, something that did sound interesting but wasn't really. And while I sat there in the corner furthest away from my mom, I realized if they were to jump another future-conversation on me right now, I couldn't get away fast enough. Besides my walking being slow, I was also in the corner furthest from the stairs. Too much time for my parents to trap me.

"So, what is Victor doing tonight?" dad asked calmly, still looking straight ahead at the tv.

"I'm not sure," I answered. "He's probably with his family." Oh please, don't let them talk during the whole film!

My mom cut in. I was pretty sure she had wanted my dad to say it, by the way she looked at him. "How are things between the two of you?"

"Fine." They didn't know I was lying. They couldn't know. He'd only said something two days ago and maybe he had changed his mind by now.

"Because if you two aren't happy anymore, it would indeed be acceptable…"

"Mom!" I gave her an angry look that left her totally unfazed. "We will not have this conversation." One more word and I would leave. Just one more.

"It's just… You haven't seemed happy lately, and if he's the reason…" I never heard my mom stammer like this.

My dad hadn't either. He saved her. "You know we like the boy. But you two are so young and if you decide he's not right for you that would be fine. You still have all your life ahead of you."

For a moment I was too stunned to do anything. Stunned because in my seventeen years in this house my dad had never talked about my relationships. Then I caught myself. This wasn't okay! I would get up and storm out. I would run up the stairs and smash the door.

Except my knee was messed up and I couldn't run, couldn't even walk properly, so all I did was limp out of the room and slowly climb up the stairs, 'till I finally reached my bedroom. And locked the door.

Chapter 25

I DID LOVE Victor. And I didn't want to lose him. So maybe pretending everything was normal would get us back to where we were a couple of weeks, even a couple of days ago. Maybe then I would be normal again.

It was almost 11pm and I had to get up at six for school. No problem. No problem at all for me. But I did want to talk to Vic, too. We've had this conversation before, though. That I shouldn't call him too late at night when we had school in the morning.

Maybe a text would be fine. Something casual, funny even. It took me some time to come up with something. And I ended up with

Me
You wouldn't believe my parents!
They think I should study math

Okay, it was neither casual, nor funny. But it didn't need immediate attention and it also wasn't something too serious.

For a moment I just sat on my bed, waiting for his response. When five minutes went by, I decided I should get changed. Out of this dress that pinched me in the waist when I sat down. And that mom wanted me to wear whenever I was supposed to look pretty.

My dearly trusted headphones were on my bedside table, so I didn't have to spend the evening in silence. Once in my pyjamas, I skipped the bathroom routine, listened to music and played on my phone until I was tired enough to sleep.

I woke up from my alarm going off, incredibly tired. The pain of sitting up reminded me of my recent accident, and when I put weight on my legs, I winced and almost fell to the ground. The pain shot through my knee into my hip. It was the worst pain I ever felt.

Thankfully, I was close enough to the bed to just fall back onto it. Then I reached for my phone.

Downstairs I heard the front door fall closed for the first time, and I texted faster. Someone I usually wouldn't. My mom.

Me

Can't go to school today. You call?

Not even a minute later she stood in the door, catching me trying to find a comfortable position. Today, even sitting felt like my bones were on fire.

Maybe she could see the pain in my face. Or maybe she remembered that this wasn't pretend, that I had really hurt myself the other day. Usually, she wouldn't just let it pass without interrogating me. Today, I was confused when she looked sympathetic.

"Your knee?"

"And my hip." Laying on my back definitely helped. Although every movement – even the tiniest – made it worse.

"I'll call the school. And the doctor. We'll go tonight." She glanced at her phone. Probably running late. "Can I leave you here alone?" Was there… *hesitation* in her voice?

I smiled at her. "Yes, I'll be fine."

She stood in my door a moment longer than necessary, looking at me all pitiful. "Call if you need anything." And then she turned away and left my door open. Before she ran out of the house though, she showed up again, a big tray in hand that we used to only touch when I was little, and we would have picnics in the backyard. "So you don't have to go downstairs for food." She also brought a bag, with loads of snacks and drinks.

"Thank you." I hadn't even thought about that yet. Surprised she had.

She put it all on my desk, and then ultimately left. I could hear her make the call to my school before she closed the front door.

I wanted to sleep, but I still had to text Vic. If everything was normal between us, he would come to pick me up. Or try to. Better not let him drive all the way here for me to not be able to open the door for him.

When I tapped on the icon to text him, I could see he had answered last night's message a few minutes ago. But it wasn't at all what I'd expected.

Vic
Maybe you should study math.
Chestwick Uni is a good school

What? I thought he knew me better than my mom! I thought he could tell I wouldn't even be able to finish one semester of math without wanting to do something else!

Calm down, Jen, I told myself. *He probably just forgot the ;) at the end.*

So, I ignored his statement.

Me
Not coming to school today

He immediately answered.

Vic
You alright?

Me
Just a little more pain
than I expected

Then he called me. I didn't think this needed more explanation.

"Hey." His voice was wonderfully soothing. Just about everything I needed right now.

"Hi." Mine was a little quieter than usual. Probably because I didn't want him to hear the pain shooting through my body displayed in my voice.

"Do you want me to stop by before school?"

"Yeah… Wait, no. I don't think I can come down to open the door."

"You sure? Can I do anything else?"

"I'm alright. I'll probably just sleep most of the day."

"Sounds good." I could almost hear him grin. "Listen…"

"Yeah?"

"Um… I'll call you from school, okay? I have to get ready."

"Okay."

"Bye, Jen."

"Bye."

It was hard falling asleep after that. My mind just kept racing through this conversation. Had he wanted to say something else? Did he want to tell me about the same thing as that night? Or was I just getting paranoid?

So paranoid in fact, I checked my phone every couple minutes.

Instead of getting a text from Vic, I got one from Lexi.

Lexi
How is my beautiful
best friend today?

Me
Great

Me
I can't move, but apart from that…

Me
Jk, don't worry

Me
But I'm in bed, not in school

Lexi
Oh Jen! What's wrong?

Me
My body betrayed me…

Me
Maybe walking around the mall yesterday was a little too much on my joints…

Me
But on the plus-side: My mom got me snacks

I hadn't come around to look into the snack-bag yet, but the way I knew my mom, it would have granola and protein bars, fruit and nuts in it. Perfectly healthy, not a lot of fun. At least she got me snacks. Baby steps.

Lexi
Great!

Lexi
But for real: how are you feeling?

Me
Okay

Me
Seriously, don't worry about me

Me
I'm about to fall asleep

Me
But I'll text you later

I really didn't feel too bad right now. I finally got a comfortable position, and my eyes were heavy, and I could easily go to sleep.

I didn't want to lie to Lexi. So I did my best to fall asleep. But only fell into some sort of half-sleep, with a bunch of weird dreams and waking up constantly.

At least I knew what to do when I got up. My dreams were sometimes guiding me to actions, and so did the last one. Vic was in it, here in my room, holding my hand. Just holding it. And it felt so good.

I wanted him to come over, but first I needed the bathroom. Could I get up? Was I able to stand up now?

No, nope, I couldn't. The pain might be less, but still too much for the whole way to the bathroom. I had to get creative.

I let myself drop to the floor – well, drop in the gentlest way I could – until I sat on my butt. With my left, still good leg I could push myself backwards, all the way to the bathroom, and then back.

Could I get downstairs like this? To open the door for Vic? And what if I fell down the stairs?

I almost let my fears stop me from texting him. Then I thought about a back door. Literally. I was pretty sure my family still kept the key for the back door hidden somewhere.

Looking at the time, I figured now was a good moment. Although he was still in class, he'd soon be at lunch. And I knew he kept his phone on silent (like all of us).

Me
Hey, can you come
over after school?

It was easier than usual to just leave the message there. Because (A) he would not answer right away, and (B) I was hungry and now had another mission to spend the time: Get to the desk where my mom had left the snacks.

I wasn't sure how to transport the tray from my desk to my bed, or even off the desk, since I needed my hands to push myself of the floor. But the bag seemed manageable.

It was the same thing as before. To the floor, backwards until I was at my destination. I put the tv remote in the bag as well, tied it and when I was back on the floor, put it in my lap.

In my bed I got into a comfortable position again. Or tried to, at least. I didn't want to lay on my back anymore, and everything else put too much pressure on my hip. Even building a mountain of pillows to keep my upper half slightly elevated was in itself painful enough. And when I finally laid on there, it wasn't as painful as sitting, but also not as painless as laying (though that wasn't entirely painless either).

After putting on a movie I was in the mood for, I grabbed some food – a granola bar and an apple – and tried not to think about all the schoolwork I was missing right now, and all the dance classes I wouldn't be able to attend.

WHEN VIC CALLED, I was fully immersed in the story on tv. Caught off guard, I answered while the movie was still on, and the lover prepared to admit his love.

"Hey," I said.

"Hi," he said. And I heard Nana yell "Hello!" in the background. Kinda cute.

"Tell Nana I said hi."

"I will. Listen, I got your text."

Again, that *Listen*. *Listen* couldn't mean anything good. *Listen* really just meant *Listen, I can't do what you asked me to do/I said.*

"Yeah, you don't have to…"

"Oh, I will come over, just a little later. I promised to drop Nana off at home, but after I'm right with you."

My heart suddenly beat faster. "Cool, awesome. You'll have to go round the house and through the back door. I think the key is under that one garden gnome that looks like Santa Clause."

He laughed. "Santa Clause, got it." In the background Nana asked "Santa Clause?" But Vic ignored her. "I'll be there as soon as possible."

The smile appeared without me having to do anything about it. "I'll save you a granola bar."

A chuckle. "Okay, bye."

"Bye."

Chapter 26

IT WAS EASIER getting him in than I thought, and at half past three, Vic was in my room, smiling like that day I almost broke my foot, running to his car in the rain after a date.

The proper way to greet me would have been 'Wow, you look like hell' since I hadn't gotten a shower or brushed my hair or put on anything but my old pink pyjamas. Instead, he said "How's your knee?"

"Hurting, as we all expected."

He sat at the edge of my bed, looking all serious now. "Has it swollen up or changed colour?"

"What, are you a doctor now?" That got a chuckle out of him.

"I might have read some articles online during arts."

"Wow, the girl you're doing this for, must be important, if you *break the rules* for her." He would never break any rules. He didn't even copy homework!

"She really is." His fingers interlaced with mine, but he was still not fully relaxed. "So? Have you put a cooling pad on your knee yesterday?"

"Nope. Rookie mistake." I should've known better. I've had injuries before, in dance that was inevitable. Cooling pads were your best friends.

"I can get you something from downstairs." Vic was about to get up, but I pulled his hand toward me.

"No, just stay here for a minute."

"It really would be better…"

"I know," I interrupted him, and pulled our hands to my mouth, pressing a small kiss on his knuckles. "Just a few minutes."

After he settled back down, I put my head on his shoulder and just stayed there for the few moments it took the guy on tv to get into a relationship with this girl, and completely mess it up. Rightfully so, she was a horrible person.

Then, unfortunately, Vic moved. "I should get you some ice," he insisted. And even me sighing loudly couldn't stop him from getting up and going downstairs to find some. Why couldn't he just stay here with me? Why did he have to fix my knee right now? (Yes, I knew, some ice wasn't going to fix it, but a few more minutes of him next to me wasn't going to hurt it either.)

When he got back, he also brought a cup of coffee. "I thought you might want some," he explained, as he put it on my bedside table. "Your caffeine addiction must be killing you right about now."

"Very true, thank you." Honestly, I had only thought about coffee three or four times today – for me, that wasn't much – but the smell made me crave some instantly.

However, I was sure I wouldn't get any until Vic hadn't looked at my knee, so I pulled my blanket aside and rolled my pant leg up. "See, not swollen, but slightly more purple than the blue it was yesterday."

The way his face was just *so serious*, made me inexplicably mad. I knew it was bad! I knew that now, not going to school, to dance or anything else could seriously hurt my future! But why did everybody have to be so serious about it? Didn't make me feel any better.

I let Vic pull the fabric over my skin, before placing the ice pack on it. My hands would have shaken too much anyway. I hid them under my blanket.

"So, what are your plans today?" I had to try to start a normal conversation. I couldn't have him investigating on how I was feeling anymore.

"Making sure you're okay," he said and sat back down next to me.

"And…?"

"I kind of want to see if your parents will kick me out when they get home." He laughed saying that. He hadn't heard the conversation I endured last night. If he had, he wouldn't laugh.

"My mom would."

"Yeah, but don't you think *this*" – he waved his hands around in the general direction of my knee – "would allow for extenuating circumstances?"

"Possibly…" I agreed. "But she wants to take me to a doctor. I don't know when and where, but she sounded very…" Concerned. I'm not sure I ever said that about my mom. At least not sarcastically.

"Maybe I can come with?"

"I don't think…"

"Well, technically, you're seventeen, so your mom is still responsible for you. But, I can help you get downstairs, and in the car, and out of the car… I mean, you want me there, right?"

"Yeah." It wasn't even a question. And he was right. Mom might be able to support me, but the stairs would be a problem. And I couldn't slide backwards on my but around the doctor's office like I'd done here, either.

"So?"

"So… Let's see what mom says. I don't want her freaking out," I decided. I squeezed his hand when I saw his disappointed look. "But I really think you coming would be good." Though I wondered where the sudden interest in helping me every second of the day came from.

Now wasn't the best time to ask that question though. It might lead to the future-talk or the 'we almost broke up before the accident'-talk, and neither of those were very delightful.

Vic didn't seem to think about that. "Good." Though the movie wasn't his genre at all, he watched all interested, you almost couldn't tell he missed the whole first half. And he seemed so relaxed, I felt like he might fall asleep any minute. Maybe he was waiting for me to cuddle up with him. But I had done nothing but lay in bed all day, and this position, though relatively painfree, got uncomfortable.

"Can you hand me the coffee?" I asked.

He grinned like he knew I was going to say that eventually. "Sure. But it's still very hot."

"You're very hot." It came out without any other thought than a quirky comeback. Because that's what Vic and I were good at. "I still want it."

Made him grin even more. "Okay, okay, be patient," he laughed, turning to the side of the bed. "Here you go."

It was a difficult manoeuvre, handling the hot coffee in bed, while half laying, trying not to spill anything on him or me. Miraculously, it worked. It was good coffee, too. I handed Vic the cup to take a sip, and then put my head on his shoulder.

When I got the cup back, I drank a little more. "You know, if I wasn't in so much pain right now, this would be a great date."

Vic didn't laugh, but he put his head on mine. "We haven't done this in a while."

My heart jumped. Yes, we hadn't. We hadn't spent enough time together at all. And this topic might just bring him back to the break-up talk.

Maybe he thought the same thing, because he was strangely quiet for the next few moments. The only noise were the stupid dialogues of that movie neither of us was really watching.

"There are some snacks in the bag." It was a weak attempt to break the silence, but somehow it worked.

"Oh yes, the promised granola bar. How could I forget?" He fished the bag from the floor and put it on his legs. His hands calmly sifted through the food items. I watched him choose one, unwrap it and put it in his mouth.

Since when didn't we have anything to talk about anymore? Was two years just the point for us when we knew everything? When the other person was so close that you didn't need to ask questions anymore? And why did it not feel like we were very close right now?

WHEN MY MOM showed up, two hours before her usual time, she was confused to find Vic there. Rightfully so. I hadn't told her, and now she probably thought that I had just stayed home to not do anything and hang with my boyfriend all day.

She didn't say anything, though. Thank the Dance Gods! Her face said enough, but I let it slide. Probably wasn't her best day either.

"Let's get ready, the appointment is in half an hour." This time, she very clearly looked at my pyjamas and my messy hair. "I'll get some coffee," she added, when she turned around. "Ten minutes,"

I didn't need a time count, since I didn't have anything else to do but get dressed and maybe take care of my hair and brush my teeth. Although it would probably be more authentic if I showed up with messy hair, since every move hurt.

"Do you need help?" Vic asked, and got up from the bed way too easily. When I tried to do the same, I almost winced in pain.

"Just hand me the shorts over there. And a bra and shirt from my closet." He threw me the pants, so they landed perfectly in my lap. Typical athlete. When he was about to hand me the red shirt with a dance pun on it ("Without dance, what's the pointe?"), I quickly intervened. "No, the black one." Mom hated shirts with words on it. She said they looked cheap and stupid. But I liked them anyway. Or maybe just because of it.

Getting dressed was easier than I thought. Thankfully I already wore underwear under my pyjama bottoms. I only needed a little help with my pants, since I couldn't lift my hip up and pull my shorts on at the same time. But in less than three minutes I was dressed and had Vic left to get me my toothbrush. I could do my hair in the car. But brushing my teeth felt necessary at this point.

Vic put my little brush in his pocket, and then helped me get downstairs. It wasn't easy, although he was really strong. But he had to carry most of my bodyweight and also not fall down the stairs himself. We made it and mom was already waiting at the kitchen counter.

She took one look at me and said "Shorts? At the doctors?"

Standing was hard enough; I couldn't take her criticism right now. "She'll have to look at my knee, won't she?"

"What about a nice skirt?"

"I thought we had to leave, mom?"

Vic was smart enough to not get in the middle of this. He already had his hands full, holding me upright.

My mom's sigh almost made me lose my temper. "Right, let's go."

She led the way to the car, and Vic followed almost too quickly. When he basically lifted me into the backseat, he groaned a little. It was easy to forget he had been hurt too.

"How's your shoulder?" I asked quietly, when he got in next to me. My mom turned the engine on and started to let her phone guide her to our destination. Not even checking if all of us were in the car yet.

"It's alright," he answered. "Though it would be easier if I could just carry you."

"Yeah, no. My pride won't allow it."

So, he had to help me all the way up the stairs to Dr Masons office. She'd been my doctor all my life, and I never questioned the positioning of her office. Well, to this day, when I could barely stay upright and wondered how people who didn't have any help were supposed to be able to see her.

The receptionist quickly pointed to the waiting area, where I could sit down while mom stayed to tell her to hurry, I'd been in pain all day. It wasn't a lie, and sitting still hurt, but I felt it kind of rude of my mom to assume everybody else didn't need an appointment as much as I did.

It only took five minutes until my name was called. And to my mom's satisfaction Dr Mason showed just the right amount of concern. We explained to her what had happened. The accident, a short hospital stay, how I could walk most of the weekend, but today it was impossible.

Dr Mason looked at my knee, and also my hip. Everything went well, until she said "Well, I agree with Dr Springsteen. Those injuries will heal by themselves, just give it time."

Mom wasn't happy with her diagnosis. "Yesterday she could still walk. Why can't she anymore?"

"I haven't seen anything that makes me think she has undetected injuries." She looked at me, and I wanted to say that yes, maybe I had just overdone it yesterday. But she continued before I could open my mouth. "However, this could be psychosomatic. Do you think that's possible, Jenna?"

"I…" didn't know. It caught me completely off guard. Not my mom though. My mom knew what to say. She always knew what to say.

"Just because you can't find anything, doesn't mean it's psychosomatic. She's been out of therapy for years now!"

I couldn't even say anything about this if I wanted to. Except that I was fine. But I wasn't sure it was true anymore.

Dr Mason smiled at my mom politely, but her words were loud and clear. "I would like to talk to Jenna alone now."

My heart skipped a beat.

"Not necessary," mom replied.

"It won't take long, but I have to ask her some personal questions, and in my experience, it is much easier for patients to answer them in private."

"But..."

"Mom," I interrupted her. "It's fine." It wasn't. "It won't take long." Hopefully.

So, she waited outside, while my heart started racing so much faster. When I got into therapy at twelve, it was the exact same thing. Although I hadn't hurt myself, we had gone to the doctors, and she had asked both my parents to step out for a minute to talk to me alone.

"How have you been feeling these past few weeks?"

"Weeks?" I repeated. "That's a long time to feel one thing."

"It doesn't have to be one feeling. You can go in as much detail as you want." Dr Mason had the incredible ability to sound friendly, respectful and professional all at the same time. Did they teach you in med school how to show just the right amount of emotion?

"The last few weeks have been good. I mean, a little stressful with final exams coming up, but okay. Nothing to worry about."

"Why do you think someone had to worry about you?"

I stared at her. Where did that come from? "Nobody has to worry about me."

"Do you think they still do? Even if they don't have to?"

"I guess…"

"Who does?"

I flushed. This became very personal, very fast. "My friends, my boyfriend… maybe my parents."

"What do they worry about?"

"My parents worry about my future, like… I have to go to a good school, get a good education, a good job. And my friends… they probably don't worry a lot."

"What about your boyfriend?"

"He… I don't know…" I couldn't even look in her eyes anymore. This must seem bad to her. "He thinks we won't make it if we're apart next year, so he wants us to go to unis that are close… I'm not sure I want that." It got out before I could think about it. Did I not want to be close to him for practical reasons? Traveling, being independent, making the best decisions unrelated to each other? Or did I feel that way because there was something else?

"What do you worry about?"

This time, I looked back up. What did I have to worry about? My future? My boyfriend breaking up? Failing all my exams? My dance career? Losing all my friends?

Why would I worry about that?

"Nothing," I said, and we both knew I was lying. But thankfully, Dr Mason didn't say anything.

"Okay, I have one last question."

What a poker face! I couldn't tell at all what she was thinking. Or feeling. I couldn't tell what I was feeling either. I should have been relieved; only one question left. But this conversation didn't help at all. There wasn't any solution to my pain, nothing about how I was supposed to survive the next few weeks if I fell behind in school and dance. "Okay."

One more question wouldn't be too bad, right?

"Do you think going back to therapy would be the right step for you?"

Chapter 27

MOM WAS FURIOUS about me not getting anything out of this doctor's visit. Well, crutches. I got crutches. So I could walk. A prescription for pain meds. But I was to only take them if absolutely necessary.

And a week off school.

Maybe to make me worry less?

Maybe because I wasn't able to go to school like this anyways?

I felt like it might be a slight nod to my mom, to leave me be, at least for those five days. Also, it was probably what I needed most. To be left alone for a little.

And I started right that night. After mom politely threw Vic out, by telling him I needed to rest so I could be better soon, we had an early dinner. My first real food for the day. Then I took my crutches and went to my room. It took me even longer than the evening of my parents telling me I was better off without Vic to get up the stairs. And I felt mom's look at me the whole time.

It was still early, but I didn't want to talk to anyone. It was so early, that dad hadn't even gotten home yet, and mom would have left for some spa treatment or fitness class if it wasn't for me.

I put my crutches next to the bed and sat down to take my bra off before laying in the same position I had been in all day. First, I texted Vic.

Me
Sorry about my mom, she can be an asshole. But thanks for coming over:)

When he didn't reply straight away – he was probably having dinner with his family or something – I pulled up Lexi's chat. *Do you think I need therapy?* I deleted that one, before I could send it.

Me
Do you worry about me? Sometimes, not right now specifically.

She didn't answer either, and when I checked the time I realized she was still in Miss Burkes' class. The earliest she could answer would be in two hours.

Good thing I still had at least fifteen tv shows on my watchlist, and about four days to watch all of them. That couldn't get boring, right?

Wrong.

Well, it wasn't necessarily uninteresting, but I found that even while watching one of my favourite shows, my mind wandered. And I didn't like it wandering. So, I tried to shut it up with games on my phone, the snacks that were still next to my bed, and texting everyone back. Nana was one of those people who always answered right away and although I didn't text her much because of that (it got very overwhelming very fast), tonight it was what I needed.

And she liked knowing gossip first hand. Apparently, everyone at school knew about the car accident Vic and I had been in, and Nana assured me that she kept telling him not to blame himself, just because he got out almost unhurt. It was the other guy's fault, who had been drinking before he got into his car.

Most of those details were news to me. About the other guy. Or that Vic blamed himself. But I didn't tell Nana that. I should probably talk to Vic about it. But then again, talking about the accident wasn't exactly on my bucket list.

I said good night when the clock struck eleven. Before I closed my eyes, I checked for replies one last time from my two most important people. Nothing. Then I fell into a not so peaceful sleep that lasted ten hours and had me waking up sweating. And so tired!

An hour later the sun shone right through my window, and my parents had long left for the day. And I felt alone.

Thankfully, my phone was already full of new messages that could distract me.

Vic's message was at the top.

Vic
Good morning, sunshine!
Hope your day is going
better than mine

Me
Why what happened?

Vic
My car broke down this morning

Vic
Although breaking down
maybe isn't the right word…

Vic
It didn't even start

Vic
Probably something with the battery

Vic
Ben had to pick me up

Me
Shit, this sucks!

Vic
Yeah

Vic
How did you sleep?

Vic
Do you feel better?

There it was. The ever so boring and annoying 'How are you?' Dodging the question was probably the best way to go.

Me
Thanks for reminding me, I'll get an ice pack if I can get up

Me
But honestly, not too bad

Me
And I dreamed like the most random stuff

Vic
Don't go downstairs by yourself!

Vic
You could fall

Vic
Isn't one of your parents home?

Me
What do you think?

Me
They'll stay home from work to sit on the couch and periodically check in on me?

Me
No

Me
And I'm happy about it

It took him a little longer to answer. Maybe because he was in school and trying to eat while keeping me company. And I was bitching about my parents. *Great job, Jen!*

Me
Please don't ask me how I'm feeling. I'm feeling like this could be the break I need or I will slowly go *crazy for not being able to move.*

This message felt like way too much. Like this was the kind of thing I shouldn't tell people, because they would think there's something wrong with me, or that I was being whiny, or weak. I didn't want to be any of those things.

My hands were shaking when I read his reply.

Vic
You're not going crazy. I'll take care of you, don't worry;)

Vic
And I'll stop, sorry

Vic
Do you want me to come over
again after school?

Vic
After practice I mean?

Me
No, my parents will be home by then

Tuesday practice took way longer than other days. Especially when they had a game on Friday.

Me
And your car doesn't work, how
would you even get here?

And I felt like being alone for a while. Hopefully not talking to anyone all day.

Vic
I could make it work

Vic
If you want me to

Now that put me in a weird position. Could I just say No? I didn't feel like company. And my parents would make sure to be around, just because I wasn't even able to reach the top drawer in the kitchen to get salt.

Me

My mom wants me to spend
time with them tonight

I lied. Lying was easier in text than in person.

Me

They probably feel guilty about
not being there last weekend.

And then I thought that it had been their choice not to come back earlier from the mountains. So maybe they didn't feel too guilty.

Me

But tomorrow, if you have time:)

Guilt wasn't exclusive to my parents after all. Not inviting him over tomorrow felt like too much.

Vic

Tomorrow it is!
Have to get back to class
now. Talk to you later!

Next was Lexi, who had already sent me about thirty texts. In none of them she asked me how I felt. Thank the Dance Gods! But by now I regretted asking her whether she worried about me. Just because of that stupid Dr Mason and her stupid questions.

Lexi
Of course I worry about you!

Lexi
You're my best friend!

I had to smile about that one. Though it felt a lot like phishing. And I hated phishing for compliments, or for reassurance or anything else. Thankfully, I didn't have to answer to that one, there were enough other messages so I could choose the most innocent ones to answer. Most were keeping me up to date on what happened during dance. Amanda falling out of a double pirouette, Penelope's tights ripping ten minutes into ballet class, and Georgia running into the mirror during jazz. New choreo, strict teachers, and people telling Lex to say Hi to me.

Me
Don't you have school right now?

Lexi
Yeah, but I finished my
assignments and mom
hasn't noticed yet

Lexi
So, what are you watching?

Me
The Nutcracker

Lexi
Barbie or Ballet?

Me
Neither

Me
It's a documentary

Me
About ballet

Lexi
Girl, take time off from dance! You'll be right in the middle of it again in no time

Lexi
Wanna watch this stupid romcom later?

Lexi
With the fish girl?

Me
You mean The Little Mermaid?

Me
And what do you mean later? You'll have dance 'till 9!

Lexi
Yep

Lexi
But I'm free between 1 – 3

Me
Won't your parents be mad about driving you to me, picking you back up, and then taking you all the way to dance?

Lexi
I thought about driving myself;P

Me
Wow! Big step!

Me
Since when are you comfortable driving?

Lexi
Since my best friend is stuck at home

Lexi
I can't just leave you there alone

Lexi
Would be cruel, don't you think?

Me
Whose car will you take?

Lexi
What's wrong, Jen? Don't
you want me to come over?

Lexi
Jen?

Lexi
You don't want me to come over?

Me
Yeah, I do

Me
Just not today
I'm really tired and shit

Me
Please don't hate me!!!

Lexi
I could never hate you!

Lexi
Just tell me if you
need anything

Me
I think I need to sleep

Me
But thanks

Me
I'll keep it in mind

Lexi
Alrighty

Lexi
Sleep well!

Chapter 28

I DIDN'T WANT to lie to Lexi, but I couldn't sleep either. Not right now at least.

Not being at school felt weird. Not going to dance later felt weird. Not moving felt weird.

But moving hurt.

Maybe it was placebo or something but standing up felt better than yesterday. Not good but better.

Also, getting to the bathroom with these crutches was easier than crawling on the floor. I mean, it was what they were for.

When I didn't text with anyone anymore, I tried to actually sleep. But now my mind had time to relive all the things I didn't really want to think about. Dr Mason for example. Well, exclusively Dr Mason, to be honest. She had asked a lot of questions, and I hadn't really thought about them at first. What they meant. Why she'd asked them. And why I had answered the way I did.

The question that bothered me the most was the last one she had asked. *Do you think, going back to therapy would be the right step for you?* It bothered me because the answer that I'd given... well, I hadn't really thought about it before I'd said no. Because that was the answer that my mom would have given. And the last thing I wanted was to actually go back to therapy and have her look at me like... like I needed therapy. And I hadn't given myself the time to actually think about the question, or whether that was something I wanted because I wasn't supposed to want it. My mom had said it: I had been out of therapy for a really long time, and I was supposed to be fine.

I was fine!

Why wasn't I fine?

This wasn't how it was supposed to go. I was supposed to stay at home and watch movies and relax and not think about things that I didn't have any control over. Things that I couldn't change anymore since I had answered Dr Mason. Now that I had said no. To a question, I wasn't sure I even wanted to think about.

Suddenly, I wished I could be at school and keep my mind on unimportant things that I wouldn't ever need to remember. Except maybe in my exams. But even those wouldn't matter in a couple of years!

Also, I didn't really have time for therapy right now. Between school and dance and studying and spending time with my boyfriend before we might just go to different colleges, places, I couldn't spend an hour a week or more in some doctor's office and talk about my shit. It wasn't important enough.

I wasn't bad enough to need therapy. No matter what anyone said.

At some point I fell asleep while watching two people go on a very boring dinner date. And I stayed in my room until my mom got home from work. And I stayed in my room until my dad got home from work. And I stayed in my room when he asked me if I wanted to have some dinner. And I stayed in my room when they went to bed.

I hadn't showered in two days, and I felt yucky. But I also knew that if I had tried to shower when my parents were there, they would have stood in front of the bathroom door to make sure I wouldn't fall, or something. After admitting to Dr Mason that I wasn't doing great last night, mom wouldn't dare let me get hurt again.

So instead, I waited until they were asleep, and I went to the bathroom to finally get cleaned up.

As it turned out, I didn't need help with *everything*. Sure, standing was hard. But I could handle it. And the warm water really helped with the pain too.

When I went to bed, I didn't think about anything. My phone had run out of battery, and I was too lazy to wait for it to turn back on. I had texted Vic and Lexi and Nana, too, in the breaks between movies today, but I didn't really feel like talking to anyone anymore.

Wednesday.

I woke up. Not well rested. Not energized. Not happy. I just woke up.

I didn't check my phone. Couldn't. Didn't do anything else either. Just laid there for a few minutes, unable to move. I closed my eyes again, trying to shut out everything that could make me feel this way. Most of it was in my head. So it didn't work.

When I got up, my body didn't hurt as much as it had the past few days, but it wasn't great, either. I still needed the crutches to get anywhere, but maybe there was hope that I could go back to dance next week.

My stomach grumbled. I looked around my room, but there was no tray of food on my desk, and only the bag with some snacks from yesterday next to my bed. I couldn't have another granola bar. Not again.

The only option was to get some food myself. I wasn't incapable of behaving like a normal human being. Even if I had needed another person to help me the last time I went downstairs. I could do it. No big deal.

The stairs were small. I had never noticed that before. Now, I had to really be careful not to put the crutches too close to the edge. It was so much work. And it took so much time.

When I finally reached the kitchen, there was nothing I actually wanted, although there was my favourite chocolate in the fridge, and I could have as many cheesy sandwiches as I wanted. But all I took were some crackers and an apple. Transportation was a problem. Of course, I could have eaten downstairs, but it didn't feel safe.

I must have looked ridiculous walking up the stairs with a bag of crackers stuck in the side of my shorts, and an apple in my mouth. But I got back to my room no problem. I ate almost all of it watching Gilmore

Girls. It was not on my watch list because I had watched it so many times before. Today I just needed a comfort series.

Half an hour later I was back asleep. I didn't think I had ever slept as much as in those past few days. But this was good. Of course, I wasn't feeling good. Sleeping helped. Or should help. It must have helped. When I woke up I was hungry again. But it was too close to my mom coming home for me to go downstairs right now. I didn't want to have to talk to her or have her watch me struggle the way upstairs. So, this was the way it was supposed to be now.

I didn't talk to anyone that day either. And when I woke up the next morning. I didn't feel any better.

Thursday.

It was raining when I finally got up. Similar to how I was feeling. Maybe I should have turned my phone back on simply to talk to someone. But I felt weak and groggy. And talking to people didn't seem manageable.

I spent the morning doing nothing. Spent the noon doing nothing. Spent the afternoon doing nothing. To the point where I was embarrassed when Lexi showed up. I was probably smelly. And not in the best mood. But she sat in my armchair like everything was normal. And started chatting about the new choreography that was just pointless. I could barely comprehend what she was saying. And my excuse?

"Sorry… I'm just really tired these days."

She accepted it. Though she looked at me for a while. Like she had a feeling that I was lying to her.

I wasn't actually lying to her. I was tired these days. But I still felt bad about it.

"I get it," she reassured me. "And I need to get going soon anyway." It was already ten. My parents didn't care if she stayed over. Or visited me. But having her being over when they were going to bed made them feel uncomfortable. And I knew that Lexi's moms certainly didn't like her staying out that late either.

"I got this new book," she told me and fumbled it out of her bag. "I'm literally in the middle of seven books, but I thought you might like it." She handed it to me. A blue cover. With red words. *How do we get over this?* I had never heard of it. But I still tried to smile. "Thanks."

I put it away. And asked Lexi to leave. Because she would have found a thousand excuses to stay if I hadn't.

Friday.

I fell when I tried to get food. Since I was home alone, I didn't have to lie to anyone about it. The thing was… I had tried to walk a few steps without the crutches, because my knee felt like it could handle the weight and my hip was almost back to normal. And I didn't fall in the kitchen when I walked around freely. As I was going back upstairs though, I slipped. I sat on the steps for a while, before I could get back up.

I didn't go downstairs for lunch.

Well, I had had breakfast at twelve, so I didn't need lunch anyway.

The day wasn't as overwhelming as the one before. Maybe because I knew I had to be normal again at night. I had promised Vic to go to his game and hang out after. He had been mad at me for not texting him about coming over on Wednesday. And for the fact that I hadn't answered any of his messages at all. But of course he didn't come out and say it. Because I had been in an accident. And apparently it gave me a free pass.

The whole *going out with friends on a Friday night* was fine with my parents. They were probably glad I would get out of the house. And took it as an okay for them to be gone yet again this weekend.

Vic had set it up so that Nana and Laurie would pick me up and make sure I was okay the whole night. He didn't phrase it that way, but I knew for a fact that Nana usually considered these games a waste of time.

I took a long overdue shower, and almost felt like a new person afterward. Put on fresh clothes, braided my hair, put ChapStick on my dry lips. With some loud music on, I stretched the first time in forever, and it felt good.

Mom and dad weren't home yet when Nana rang the doorbell. She had announced herself five minutes ago in a text, so I'd had some time to get downstairs, very carefully. And without my crutches.

"Hi," Nana squeaked, and pulled me into a tight hug.

I was a little proud to get to the car on my own. It was almost too easy. And I was happy to get to sit down again. Laurie had her car still running and welcomed me with the biggest smile. “I’m so glad you’re better!” she said.

“Me too,” I replied. And I almost believed it.

Chapter 29

I WOULD HAVE loved to say hi to Vic before the game, and wish him good luck, but all I could do was text him. After we sat down on the cold bleachers a little further up ("The best view in the house," Nana had said), I couldn't get down again. Well, I probably could, but I needed to conserve my energy.

The game was good, and Nana and Laurie were nice company. They both acted as if doing this was completely normal. Yes, Laurie and I had sometimes watched these games together, but usually just as a pre-party thing, and not with Nana who cheered for the boys like there was no tomorrow. It looked like they could hear her, even from up here – at least that's what I thought when two of them looked up to us.

Nana had brought snacks, Laurie drinks. And although Nana made fun of Laurie for bringing non-alcoholic stuff, she drank at least three cans of coke and ran to the toilet as soon as the game was over. Which left Laurie to make sure I got down the bleachers okay.

As my experience had showed, getting down wasn't the dangerous part, so I tried chatting like everything was normal. Still, we waited for most of the people to leave instead of letting them accidently push us.

When we caught up with Nana, she already waited at the exit where the boys would come out any minute. She was randomly talking to people from her classes walking by. Grimaced when they left. Did she just do it to show how popular she was?

"Hey, all good?" Nana asked me, as Laurie and I approached her.

"Yeah, fine."

If we went a few more steps outside, we could sit down. And not every person exiting would walk right past us. But we didn't. Because I didn't say any of it out loud. All these people, some of them staring at me, made me feel uneasy. I focussed on the door to the team changing rooms, willing Vic to come out, but it took a good ten minutes before he did.

"Hi!" He hugged Nana first, then a shy Laurie, who was actually just looking over his shoulder to see if Ben was there yet. Lastly, he pulled me into a tight hug and planted a kiss on top of my head. I felt something warm in my chest almost instantly. Yes, this was exactly what I needed.

I was ready to go home, but Nana didn't like the idea. "No, we're going to Matthews party. I mean, we won and you're all better. There's a lot to celebrate!"

Maybe she was right. Maybe this should be celebrated. Maybe I shouldn't hide in my room anymore. "Okay…"

"Don't worry," Nana stage whispered. "You can go with your loverboy, we'll take Ben."

This wasn't at all what I'd been expecting. I mean, I knew that Vic always took Ben to the games, and car swapping wasn't so farfetched, and normally I wouldn't mind…

I didn't want to make a scene, but the closer I got to the car, the more nervous I felt. Did nobody remember I had had an accident in this very car?

I didn't say anything when Vic held open the door, just let myself drop on the all too familiar seat. Damn! If I could have screamed out loud, I would have. Something like *Why can't I be normal?!* But Vic had already rounded the car and sat down in the driver's seat, looking at me for a little as if he wanted to say something. He didn't. He got settled, and then smiled at me. It didn't reach his eyes though.

"Are you okay?"

I wanted to tell him, yell at him, to stop asking me that and also say *No, I'm not*, but when I opened my mouth, nothing came out.

He took my hand right then, interlaced his fingers with mine, but I pulled away. I couldn't. Couldn't pretend I was fine.

Instead of saying all that, I replied "You need both hands to drive." And it came out a lot rougher than I intended to.

"Put your seatbelt on, then." Thankfully, he didn't even look at me, and focussed on the car. Once I buckled in, he started the engine.

There were so many things I wanted to say. I was fine, he didn't need to worry about me, I was just tired, and it would all be okay. All of them were lies of course. And none passed my lips.

I couldn't tell him, how my whole body was on fire, sitting in his car. His car that was once my safe space. I couldn't tell him that every second I was in here, I wanted to jump out and run until my feet bled. Or until my knee was permanently damaged. And I would never tell him that I'd been fine sitting in Laurie's car. And in mom's car. That this was the only one that made me want to do bad things.

When we finally made it to Matthew's house, well, the end of his street, I had to hide the fact that I was shaking. Pretend like everything was normal. As if I was cold, I pulled my arms around myself, and started walking.

Walking helped. My heart rate slowed; the shaking stopped. We were almost at the house when Vic touched my arm. "Hey, can we talk for a second?"

"Now?" My glance went from the house our friends already had entered, to him, now standing still, next to all the cars parked on the side of the road.

"Why not now?" He ran his hand through his hair, more annoyed than nervous. "We really need to talk."

"Okay," I said, although it did not feel okay. "Let's screw the party and talk." I couldn't help but take a step back, staring at him expectedly, which must have looked as if *I* was annoyed, because he visibly clenched his jar.

I kind of hoped we could actually skip the party. I wasn't feeling like partying anyway, but then again, going back inside his car wasn't an option.

"Jen, I really don't think… I don't think we can keep going like this."

I had to push my fingernails into my palms to stop myself from shaking. Or doing anything stupid. The pain helped with that. And with keeping my head somewhat clear. "What do you mean by 'this'?"

He didn't answer. But I already knew anyway.

"Do you want to break up with me?" And this time I couldn't stop a big tear from rolling down my face.

He really didn't see it at all, did he?

Chapter 30

"NO," HE SAID quickly. "I don't want us to break up. I want us to fix this."

I believed him. I had to believe him.

"But, you see…" He took my hand, squeezing it way too hard. And then he let go right away to fold his arms across his chest. "I really don't want us to spend even less time together… but spending time with you is hard. You're never really around, and when you are, Lexi is there too."

I wanted to say something. Nothing came out. This was like the break-up-talk all over again. Only thing left was a car crushing into me.

"It feels like you don't care about me anymore. We don't really see each other out of school, you're always at dance. And even when you could invite me to have coffee with your dance friends, you don't. I don't get it."

It was like he didn't even remember we'd had this talk before. Or maybe he didn't think I remembered?

"They'd make fun of me." It was true. But I could see he didn't believe me.

Heard it in his voice, too. "For having a boyfriend?"

"Some dancers are... weird." Some thought you weren't focussed enough on dance when you had a boyfriend. Which made you bad and the team worse.

He didn't get it. "What about all the times you're dragging Lexi along when the two of us could spend time together? Every single party we go to..."

"She's not here now, is she?" He was kind of right, though. I did bring Lexi a lot. Because I liked spending time with her. Was that so bad?

"No, but you're texting her every two seconds. And let me guess, once we're in there," he pointed to Matthew's house, "you will find your friends and play drinking games."

"I'm not drinking tonight." Wow, stupid. I should have said something like *I didn't want to come here today* or even *We can spend the party together*. It would have sounded better. Probably wouldn't have changed anything though.

"What are you going to do then?"

Why did he have to use this tone with me? Wasn't it enough that we were fighting with all of our friends just a few minutes away. "I didn't even want to come here, Vic!" There it was. "But if you want to, we can stick together tonight. Just say something, don't make such a big deal out of it!"

"That's just it, Jen! You never tell me you want to be around me. It feels like I have to force you to spend time with me!"

"We're in a relationship! Do I really need to spell it out, that I actually want to spend time with you?" This was horrible. And getting worse by the minute.

"How would I know when you never say anything? We haven't even had sex in months."

"That's not true!" The last time was just last week. A few days before the accident. Granted, we have had to plan it two days in advance, and were done after ten minutes, but it happened.

"If you count car sex."

I definitely counted it. There was a time when we only did it in the car. On purpose. Back then it was new and hot and forbidden. Now it was just about the only place we could do it. We couldn't go to his house because of his parents, not to mine because Mom had a habit of getting off work early whenever we tried. "I don't know what to say to that." Without sounding like a jerk. "And maybe this isn't the right place to talk about it."

"It never is."

"I didn't say that." If I was honest, I knew where he was coming from. If we couldn't even make time for sex outside a car, then how could we ever talk? Really talk. But still, with all our friends just a few steps away, this was the last place I wanted to do this. "Is it too much to ask to have this conversation in private?"

He didn't answer. Because – just as I had predicted – someone interrupted us. Someone with the name Nana. "Are you guys coming or what?"

"Yeah," Vic said instantly.

Okay, conversation over. Got it.

"Go ahead," I said, although he was already on his way. "I have to call my mom back."

Both Nana and Vic stopped for a second, probably wondering whether they could leave me alone after just having had an accident last week, but then simultaneously decided that yes, I should stand out here alone for a bit.

Maybe Vic had known that I was lying, but weirdly enough, when I looked at my phone, there was indeed a voice message from my mom. I turned my back to the party, before lifting the phone to my ear to listen to it.

"We're on our way to Livre Hotel for your dad's Christmas present now. The website said there might be bad reception, so I sent you the hotels number. We'll be back Monday morning. See you then!"

Usually, I wouldn't even have gotten a message like this, even if they were difficult to get to for two days. I guess now things were different.

When I entered the house, I could see Vic talk to Ben, Nana and Laurie. So much about *me* hanging out with my friends without him. My urge to not talk to them led me into the kitchen. Screw the *I'm not going to drink tonight*. When it started like this, maybe some alcohol would lighten my mood.

Unsurprisingly, I met Matthew Anderson himself in the kitchen, pouring some colourful liquids into different cups while sitting on the kitchen counter.

"Jenna!" he shouted cheerfully, jumping to the floor. "Good to see you!"

"Hi!" I couldn't match his energy. Not even if I hadn't been in a fight just minutes ago. "Can you get me a drink?"

"Sure, my love, what do you want?" His good mood was kind of infectious.

"What do you recommend?"

"The best for the best: My personal take on Caipirinha!" He held a cup under my nose which definitely had more alcohol in it than the regular cocktail.

"Maybe something that won't make me dance on tables in fifteen minutes?"

"I think everyone here wants to see you dance on tables." He winked at me, before turning around to look for a different drink. He chose one of the cups which already had something blue in it, and filled it up with orange juice. "Ta-da! Swimming pool, weak-ish for the lady."

"Thanks Matthew."

I was about to leave the kitchen, when he called after me. "And remember, you don't have to be drunk to dance on tables!"

The good mood quickly changed when I got to the living room and couldn't see Vic or any of my friends anymore. I wasn't actively looking for him, just casually observing my surroundings, but he wasn't where he had been just minutes ago. And my brain noticed.

Stupid brain.

Didn't Vic want to spend time with me? Wasn't that his whole argument? That we didn't have enough time together and Lexi was always in the way? Well, Lexi wasn't here right now, and Vic was nowhere to be found either.

Paul Douglas was there though. And he pretended like he hadn't seen Vic here, and like he didn't know we were dating. Instead, had the audacity to flirt with me.

While Matthew calling me 'my love' was all friendly and not at all creepy, I felt nothing but uncomfortable around Paul Douglas. His hands were literally sticky when he tried to get me to dance with him, and he looked at me in this weird, drunken, flirty way. "Jen, huh. You know, I think you're very hot. I've always thought that."

"Let me go, Paul."

He didn't. On the contrary. His hand tightened around mine. "You know, when I heard about Victor and Nana, I thought to myself… I thought… you're so much better. You are so much better! Why would he choose her? But I guess good for me."

Instead of acknowledging his words, I tried to free myself. "You're drunk, Paul. Leave me alone."

He didn't. And my hand started stinging. "He didn't deserve you. He really didn't. I can be good for you, Jen. Believe me, I will be so good to you."

"What are you even talking about?"

"Victor and Nana, you know? The holding hands, the secret dates, you know? Oh wait… you don't know."

He freed my hand, and I took the chance to take a few steps back. "Actually, I don't even want to know." Not from you, anyway.

"But…"

I left before he could grab my hand again, but his words didn't leave me. What did he mean there was something going on between Vic and Nana? When where they holding hands? Going on dates? Was it while I was at home and in pain? And Nana! Of all people! The girl who would be my best friend at school if I had a best friend at school. Her, Laurie, Ellie and I always hung together during breaks and classes. No way she and Vic… had something.

Nana probably wouldn't keep it to herself anyway. She loved talking.

And even though we had just been fighting outside, Vic wouldn't do this to me.

No, this was probably just some fucked up gossip.

Damn, I needed Lexi to be here right now! But she had a date, so even texting her was not an option.

It was the start of a big party, but it was already way too loud. Most were drinking, some were drunk. And it was not as much fun as usually, without my friends or Vic.

I pushed myself through the crowd and started wandering toward the dark corner of the living room. The one that was usually reserved for drinking games, but this early in the night untouched.

I walked around, not wanting to stay in any place too long, in case someone took it as an opportunity to talk to me. I didn't really want to talk. Not to anyone.

Just as I questioned whether it would be a catastrophic idea to sneak out and go home on my own (by bus maybe?), I realised my purse with my keys, money and everything else was still in Vics' car. Fuck. There was nothing I could do but talk to Vic. And I knew he didn't want to talk to me anytime soon. Pretty obvious by him and everyone else abandoning me as soon as I walked in.

At least I had my phone with me. The batterie might be low, but someone at this party must have had a charger, right?

I wished I could text Lexi. She would know what to do. Or she would at least tell me I wasn't in the wrong here. Cheer me up. Honestly, I found it kind of strange that my friends were so adamant about me being here, checking on every step I took at the game, just to leave me alone as soon as we came here. Was this some plot against me? Some game they made up? *Let's see how Jen gets out of this one! This will be funny!*

Fuck them. I didn't have the nerve to play games right now. The urge to leave this mess of a party got bigger and bigger with every passing second.

They weren't even looking for me. They didn't even care if I got hurt again. They dragged me here to watch me fail.

Woah, stop Jen. Let's not fall into this deep pit of angst. Not here. Not when all these people are around.

Three deep breaths. One. Two. Three.

Didn't help.

But maybe another drink would.

Funny how I'd promised Vic today of all days I wouldn't drink, and it was the first time in forever since I craved one. It made me feel lighter somehow. And that's what I needed right now. To not let the heaviness consume me.

When had I finished my drink? Was I really this nervous? I couldn't remember. And I didn't feel any of the alcohol yet.

Matthew was still in the kitchen, mixing drinks for people. He turned to me with a smile, which was odd because we didn't really know each other. But then again, I really needed this right now. Someone to be nice to me.

"Another weak Swimming Pool for you, my love?" Somehow, his British accent suited him. And it calmed me down.

"No, I need something strong."

His eyebrows shot up ever so slightly, and he nodded with a bright grin. "Good to have you on the dark side, Jen. You feel like orange juice again?"

"Sounds good." I didn't really care. It wasn't like I had a favourite drink. I didn't drink enough for that.

When he handed me a Tequila Sunrise (I didn't know it was made with orange juice), I thanked him smiling and turned around. This time, there were enough other people in the kitchen, so Matthew didn't strike up another conversation.

I only took two steps out of the kitchen, when a guy a lot taller than me bumped into my shoulder, spilling the leftovers of his drink and some of mine onto my shirt.

"Shit! I'm so sorry," Ben said.

I couldn't help but curse loudly, even though I knew Ben was the last person to do something like this on purpose. Even if he was on Vic's team and one of his closest friends, he wouldn't intentionally pour smelly, sticky liquid over my front.

Of course Ben tried to help, but all I wanted was get to the next bathroom and take this shirt off.

Which is what I did, without even turning to talk to him again. Only, when I was close enough to the downstairs bathroom to see there already was a line of five girls waiting to get in. I changed my mind. There was one upstairs – actually there were two, but there was one pretty hidden – where people usually didn't go this time of the night.

Up the stairs (carefully, of course), to the right. The far end of the long hallway. The light wasn't even turned on – in a house where no light was ever turned off. So I had some privacy. It was just as luxurious as it could get. All black and white, huge spaces, clean and modern.

When I caught a glimpse of myself in the large mirror, I grimaced. Besides the shirt, my hair also hadn't stayed in my ponytail, with stray strands flying everywhere. My mascara was a little smudged and you could see my bra's outline through the damp shirt. It wasn't white, thankfully, but light enough with its beautiful pastel green, so the blue of the fabric underneath could shine through.

The door was locked as I put my drink by the side of the sink and peeled my shirt off. The sports bra was one of my prettiest. The kind you could wear by itself. With laces and a subtle pattern of flowers. Honestly, I had put it on because I thought Vic and I would be alone at some point tonight. Before there was any chance we'd go to a party neither of us were really in the mood for.

The liquid hadn't drenched the material fully, so I opted to splash some water on it and me, in hopes it wouldn't be as sticky. Maybe I could jump in the pool later. Nobody would notice.

Could I get out though? With my knee and hip still wobbly, there was no way of knowing. And I sure as hell wouldn't want some strange guy trying to 'help' me.

I didn't like what I saw in the mirror. You could still see traces of the accident on my body, and I felt way too exposed. But there was no use in staying in here all night. Though I thought about it. I needed to find Vic, make him open his car for me, so I could get my stuff and leave.

If my phone's battery weren't flashing angrily at me, I would just text him. Just my luck! I took another sip from my drink, before I gathered all my courage and left the bathroom. Staying in here even longer wouldn't do me any good.

As expected, I didn't see any of my friends. It was like we weren't even at the same party. People bumped into me. Some on purpose, some not. It hurt either way. With every contact, my unease got bigger.

Maybe I could just walk home, break in through a window?

The neighbours would probably call the police though. Even if they recognized me, they didn't like me or my parents enough to let it slip.

After what felt like the fiftieth guy bumped into me and eyed me like he wanted to devour me right then and there, I took escape in one of the bedrooms upstairs.

Chapter 31

I HAD SAT down in front of the bed, leaning against its frame, and was close to crying when the door opened.

Shit. Shit. Shit!

The last thing I needed right now was a drunk horny couple stumbling in here, having sex on the bed behind me. They wouldn't even notice I was here, and I would be the creep for making myself known. Or pathetic for crying alone in a bedroom at a party.

I couldn't move, though. All I could do was watch the door open, almost in slow motion. Fear creeping up my spine.

It was Vic. Vic! Charging in there as if there was something to see. Something unpleasant. Something like… me cheating?

That's what he was thinking, when his eyes darted toward the top of the bed first before they found me on the floor in front of it.

"Jen!" His voice was rough. Raspy. Had he been drinking?

No. When he sat down next to me, I could smell it. Or not smell it. There was no trace of alcohol in his breath when he spoke. "What are you doing here?"

"I believe it was you who dragged me to this party." I sounded way sassier than usually. Because I was way more pissed than usually.

He sounded way angrier too. "I mean here. In this bedroom. Is anyone with you?" He looked around, toward the adjoining bathroom I hadn't even noticed yet.

"Who would be with me?" I was almost laughing. But this wasn't funny.

"Where is your shirt?" His piercing eyes landed back on me, and I wished they were looking for my imaginary lover again.

"Do you really want to know or…?" I didn't finish. I couldn't say it out loud. "You know what? I don't even care. You want to break up with me? Do it. But don't accuse me of sleeping around or some shit. You were the one who dragged me here, and then left me alone. I just need my stuff out of your car and then I'm gone."

"Fuck, Jen. What are you talking about?" He looked at me like he was actually clueless! Like he hadn't tried to break up with me before the accident, and then again just a couple hours ago. It made me feel even shittier. Because either he was lying, or I was imagining things.

"You left me alone the whole night, Vic," I whispered. "Why would you do that after what happened last week?"

I didn't think I would actually bring the accident into this conversation, but I guess I was surprising myself today. I also didn't think I would try to break up with Vic.

When he didn't answer – I couldn't really blame him – I continued. "I want to go home, Vic. My keys are in your car, so you'll just have to let me get them and…"

"I'm not going to let you leave alone." He looked at me like I was crazy for suggesting it. Then his features softened. His voice too. "But we've only been here two hours."

I was ignoring the fact that 'letting me do' anything sounded very much like I couldn't take care of myself, when that's what I'd been doing all my life. "My friends have not so much as looked at me once. But you know who did? Just about every other guy at this party. By now everyone has heard about the accident. I feel like a zoo animal. I just want to go home."

"Let's go then." He got up gracefully and held his hand out to pull me up too. I took it. Maybe I was overreacting. Maybe he hadn't tried to break up with me, and I'd just seen things that weren't there.

We made our way downstairs and through the party people, only stopping once when Nana showed up out of nowhere. She forced a smile when looking at me, before exchanging a few quick words with Vic.

Wait a second! Was this imaginary too?

I relaxed when we finally stepped outside. It felt like I could breathe again after being squished in that house forever.

We didn't talk when we walked to the car. Or when we got in. Or when we were driving. But I couldn't have talked in there either way. It felt like the world had turned into ice (or was it just me who couldn't move?), and acid was running through my veins. I felt like passing out but willed myself to focus on the night sky. There were a few stars. Actually, just one. And it wasn't dark enough to be black, but very dark blue. The kind of dark blue you see in pictures of the night sky...

It wasn't a long drive to my house, and I was relieved when Vic got out with me, so he couldn't see how my legs were shaking. I pressed my hand against my hip while taking the three, four, five steps to the front door. Put the key in, turned it. It was dark inside, much darker than outside.

Vic didn't step in with me.

The shaking didn't fade. I could feel my heart racing.

My hand found the light switch just as Vic declared "I'm going back to the party, call me if you need anything."

I looked at him, only to see he'd already turned away from me.

"Actually, can you stay?" It stopped him in his tracks. "Just a couple of minutes..." My voice was shaking a little, too. I couldn't be alone right now. If I were a liar, I would tell Vic I needed him here. Truth was, I just needed someone.

Maybe he sensed it. I was still shocked when he squinted at me and said "I can't. I promised Nana to be back and take her home later."

I didn't argue. I didn't have it in me. It broke me.

I let him leave. Closed the door and locked me in with my fears and my ever-shaking body.

Just breathe, Jen. One, two, three.

At least my head was clear enough to notice the phone in my pocket and the charger in my purse.

The display wouldn't turn on right away, and waiting was torture. All I could do was breathe and all I had to do was breathe. When I finally got back to my home screen, I knew better than to text someone who wouldn't care.

Me

How's your date going?

Lexi

Really good!

Lexi

She's so amazing, I'm
almost drooling

Lexi

What are you doing tonight?

I couldn't.

I couldn't ruin her night, too.

I needed a friend, but I also needed to be a friend. Which meant not interrupting Lexi on what sounded like one of the best dates she ever had.

Was it selfish of me to still want her here?

I was a terrible friend. A terrible person. My own boyfriend didn't even like me enough to stay. My friends didn't want to be around me, and Lexi had found someone better.

I was going to die alone.

Alone and in pain.

I DIDN'T KNOW when I had started crying. Or curling up on the floor. But my phone was on the counter, and I was down here, feeling like my heart would implode any second.

I couldn't breathe…

I couldn't breathe…

Couldn't breathe…

Couldn't breathe…

Couldn't breathe…

I didn't know how long I'd been laying there. Didn't know how long I'd stayed in this hell. Too long. Too damn long. My ears were ringing.

Ringing.

Ringing.

The doorbell.

Not my ears, the doorbell.

Should I open it?

Could I open it?

My body felt numb. Like it wasn't even my own. Like it wouldn't do what I asked it to do when I would try.

It rang again.

Someone was knocking.

I should open it.

I couldn't stand up.

My face was numb from crying.

My muscles were too tense to move.

Ringing. Knocking.

I was pathetic.

Chapter 32

I DIDN'T KNOW how. Or why. Or when I had finally opened the door, but when I did, it was Lexi, wide-eyed.

"Jen? Are you okay?"

What a stupid question, seeing as I could barely stand upright or breathe properly.

She didn't wait for an answer though. Didn't even stop to close the door, when she pulled me into a tight hug. "It will be okay," she told me, gently leading me to the couch.

She left, and I sunk into the cushions. It wouldn't be okay. How could it be okay?

Lexi returned, a cold compress in hand. "Take this." She held it against my wrist, letting go, when I held it on my own. Then she put an arm around my shoulders. "What happened tonight?"

I couldn't. Couldn't form the words to tell her everything. But maybe I could tell her something.

"Vic and I are over. He doesn't really care anymore."

"Fuck, Jen…"

"I asked him to stay and he left." Tears started falling again. If it were anyone else but Lexi, I wouldn't have let them pour out like that. Neither my tears, nor my thoughts. But this was my best friend. The Kaycee Rice to my Sean Lew, the peanut butter to my jelly. There were no secrets between us. Well, almost none.

I felt my heart slow down, despite my feelings overwhelming me, and Lexi could feel it too. "He doesn't deserve you," she told me.

At some point we went upstairs – though I credited most of it to Lexi. All I did was let her lead me. She put me in the shower, and I hated to admit that the cold water made me feel better. Calmer somehow.

She got me into clean and comfortable clothes. She put me in bed. She turned off the big light but left on the small one on my desk. Then she snuggled up next to me, her hand on mine, her warm eyes fixed on me.

"You know you can talk to me, right?"

I knew. And yet, I didn't. Hadn't. Felt like I couldn't.

Or at least that's what I'd been thinking. The words came out without any stopping them. "It's just... no one can save me."

It was like she was expecting this. Lex didn't even think before answering "Because you can save yourself." She said it so matter-of-factly that I almost believed her straight away. "You're one of the strongest people I know. You might need, or want, someone to hold your hand," she tightened her fingers around mine, "but you do not need to be saved. You need someone to tell you you are loved. You are wanted. You are needed. You are amazing. You're talented. You're special. You're smart. You're real. You're warm. You are my best friend. All those things. And so much more. And even if you don't need to be saved, I'll still be here, to catch you if you fall."

Now the tears really fell. "I love you, Lex." It was barely more than a whisper, but it was all we needed.

"I love you more," she replied whole-heartedly.

And while I fell asleep, Lexi stayed there, not letting go.

Chapter 33

IT FELT LIKE an eternity later. Or maybe just a few minutes. Nothing in-between.

I was still in bed, Lex still next to me. My breathing was slower than it had been in hours, and I felt a relaxing level of tiredness. I was ready to fall back asleep, when I heard Lexi talk. To herself? To me?

She was on her back, staring up at the ceiling. Her hand still wrapped around mine. The warm glow of my desk lamp cast a small shadow on her chin.

"...Then she ordered two different kinds of fries – cheese and sweet potato – and we split both, which was awesome. Ketchup got on her nose, and she wasn't embarrassed at all, just really cool and amazing and funny. And then the server spilled half her lemonade on her, and she was so cool about that too. Like nothing could faze her. And when I asked her, she told me life was too short to get mad about the little things. There was something so honest and wild and free about her..."

It took me a moment to realize she was talking about her date tonight. And it made me happy, hearing how happy Lexi was. I closed my eyes and listened to her voice telling me – or, well, the ceiling – about the great night she'd had.

"I like, fell instantly in love with her. And so did the waitress. And the people on the next table who were like listening in the whole time. And after that we went to that diner club, the one across the street from JustDanceThings, just as they turned the main seating area into a dance floor, and this crazy DJ showed up, it was really amazing. If my moms had seen me there, they'd flipped. I was of course wearing the red top that's super cute when you're sitting but a little loose, and I almost flashed about ten people. It was such a fun night, but the whole time I kept thinking what you were doing and how you were probably still in pain from the accident, and how the night would have been even more fun with you.

And I know that's not a nice thing to think, because Avery is great. She is like the sweetest and coolest girl I ever went out with… but she's just not you."

The silence hung over us like a cloak. I didn't dare breathe.

If I had known that's where the story was going, I would've tried to fall back asleep, or made her aware I was up, or something. She didn't really want me to hear it. And I felt like I had invaded her privacy by being awake.

Lexi sighed a few times, and I kept so still, I fell asleep again quicker than I'd thought.

Chapter 34

THE NEXT MORNING, I woke up when Lexi climbed over me to get out of bed. I heard the bathroom door close and open again a few moments later, and when she came back into my room, she stopped somewhere close to the door.

"Good morning, princess."

Her smile was so genuine, I wasn't even sure last night really happened. But it had happened, I could see the neatly stacked pile of clothes from the party on my desk chair. It was how Lexi took care of me. Organizing my clothes. The blue sports bra right on top.

"Morning," I replied, smiling. "Do you want coffee?" If I didn't get out of bed now, I wouldn't today. I let my feet drop to the floor, and noticed how much better my knee felt.

"You bet I do."

We went downstairs, chatting away, when my mind wandered to a memory that maybe was a memory or maybe had been a dream. I wasn't sure. "I forgot to ask: How was your date last night?"

"Really good." She didn't give any hint whatsoever whether what I had heard last night was something she had actually said. "Avery is very fun."

"You like her?"

"I do."

AND MAYBE IF she had stayed that day, I would have been fine. But I sent her away, thinking I was better. That nothing would shake me the way it had last night.

But it did.

And when I started thinking, about what it would mean, if Lexi had actually said those words for real, I got scared. So I was good enough as best friend, but not enough to be more? So she could text me all day, talk to me all night, but I wasn't someone to be serious about?

I was stressed out enough about this revelation, but when Vic started calling, I couldn't hold it in anymore. Good thing my parents were still gone. Good thing all I had to do to be alone was not leave the house.

But that phone!

In-between his calls and texts, my display told me about Lexi's messages. One or two were from Nana and Laurie, too. I was bombarded. And I couldn't hold up the ford.

Truth be told, if Lexi were still here, I would have been better. If she were still here, I could breathe. Ignore my phone. Be normal. Just be a fucking normal girl.

If Lexi had stayed, I wouldn't have filled the bathtub with excruciatingly cold water. I wouldn't have dropped my phone in. And I wouldn't have gotten in after, letting the water consume me.

For everyone who's here for the drama: this is your ending. This is the story.
And for everyone who needs closure: I got you.
This is not the end; you're okay.

Chapter 35

I WAS IN Mina's room again, but it had changed somehow. The toys were gone, replaced with décor, books and instruments. The baby bed was now a big one, the pink had faded, and Bubblegum, the teddy bear, sat alone on one of the bookshelves. But my rug was still in the same place, and Mina was there too.

Except it wasn't the Mina I'd known. This was a grown up Mina, probably about my age. She smiled at me when she sat down in her spot at the edge of the rug. "Did you see it?" she asked.

I knew exactly what she meant. What she had meant all along.

How I'd died.

"No but," I stuttered, the realization diminishing my ability to think. "Why am I back here?"

"So you didn't see it." Mina looked disappointed. She pulled her legs in like she had done when she was five. "I thought after all this time…"

But she didn't say what she had thought, and I waited for her to continue, but she didn't. "What happened?" I finally got out.

"You know I can't tell you. You have to find that out yourself."

"No, yes. I mean to you? What happened to you?"

She smiled then, but it was a sad smile. "That's not important."

"It is to me. What happened?"

"I grew up. And I can assure you, you played a big part in that."

"How? I wasn't even here?"

"Not physically maybe, but you were always there."

"Why are you so sad?"

"Because I have to let you go now. You have to go back."

"I don't want to go back. There's so much pain." Just thinking about how my boyfriend didn't love me enough, how my best friend didn't love me enough, how I didn't love me enough, brought the tears back to my eyes.

"I know. But it's the right thing to do. You haven't been to Paris yet, or danced in a musical, or fell in love with a stranger."

"That wasn't on my list." I giggled. Why did I giggle? This was not the right time.

"But it will be." She sighed, as her expression turned serious again. "There's so much you still need to do."

"How do you know?"

She didn't answer. "You have to find out what really happened. And you have to find out how to wake up."

"I am awake."

"Not here. In your world."

Chapter 36

THE WATER HAD calmed my heart rate enough I could actually think for once. And I finally knew.

I didn't want to do this anymore. I didn't want the pain and the suffering and the anger I felt when I realized I should be happy. I didn't want people to tell me I was fine when it was only what they wanted me to be.

I wanted to be okay. But I wouldn't be while I was still here. In this place, in this time, in this life.

I needed better. I needed more. I needed to make decisions for myself. Even if it meant breaking more than I was healing.

My phone, like most phones, could handle some water. I had no trouble turning it back on. It instantly flooded me with all the texts I hadn't answered yet.

And a call I didn't expect.

Lexi.

"I feel like we need to talk," she said without hesitation, or even a greeting. "Do we need to talk?"

"I don't know." *Liar.* "Do you want to talk?"

Why did I do it? Why couldn't I just say what I thought? Why couldn't I just do what I promised myself I would do?

"Jen?"

I had to make a decision here. About the person I wanted to be. About how I would take care of myself.

It wasn't that hard. I could do it. I could do it. I could do it. "Lex? I want to talk but I have to do something else first."

It took me all of five minutes to text Vic to meet me at the park down the street from my house, and to get his confirmation. I wanted to do this sooner rather than later.

When I went through my room I grabbed all of the stuff he had left here at some point or another. Notebooks, a Bluetooth speaker, and the sweater I had borrowed a year ago. I loved that sweater. But it wouldn't be a break if I kept parts of him.

I didn't bother taking care of my hair. Or the perfect outfit. It didn't matter.

My hair was still damp, and I put it in a bun (typical ballerina). And you could see some of my bruises from the accident and from before when I was wearing shorts and a t-shirt, but I didn't care.

At least that's what I told myself when I left the house to meet Vic. It was roughly a ten-minute walk, and the bag in my hand felt strange. I should have put his stuff in a rucksack or something. Would have been much more comfortable to carry.

There was barely anyone around, and still I felt like people were staring at the red and blue and purple of my skin. Fresh and old bruises. Scary big ones, and those too small to notice from a distance. But in my mind, they could see all of them. Made me a lot more uncomfortable than if I had just worn Jeans. In a 30° summer heat.

Vic was already waiting for me when I got there. Casually leaning against the side of his car. No sign of tiredness. Maybe he had left the party early? Or maybe he was just too perfect to be true.

“Hey, you alright?” he asked, a worried look on his face.

I couldn’t say *Yes*, I couldn’t even say *I try to be*. Both of them would have been lies. “I have your stuff,” I said instead, handing him the bag.

He didn’t take it. Just looked at me puzzled. “What do you mean?”

“We should break up,” I blurted out. And his look made it clear I needed to soften the blow. “Not because I don’t love you anymore, and not because I have feelings for somebody else and not because you may have something going on with Nana – I’m not mad, I promise – but because we are growing up and we need to go our own ways and they’re not leading in the same direction right now. I don’t regret anything, and I want you to know that, because we were right when we were together, but time changes things, time changed us, and we need to let it change.”

“Okay.”

“Okay?” Was that all? Was that everything our two-and-a-half-year relationship boiled down to? *Okay*?!

"Yeah, okay. I mean, doesn't make sense trying to save it if you don't want me to save it, right?"

"Huh." Yes, it actually made sense.

"And I didn't do anything with Nana. I would never as long as we're together."

Hm. So Paul Douglas really had been too drunk to know what he was talking about. "That's very gentleman of you," I said unironically.

And he replied "No, it's the bare minimum. I swear if you let the next guy tell you not cheating is difficult, I will have to step in."

"You still want to be in my life?"

It wasn't even a question. "Sure, if you let me."

"Definitely. Believe it or not, I didn't just date you for your good looks and athleticism."

"You didn't date me at all for my looks and athleticism." Back then he had been a gawky 15-year-old who'd rather go to the park and play basketball with his friends, than to the gym to work on the height of his jumps. Plus, I once told him I didn't care about his muscles as long as he had a good heart.

"Right, I dated you for your knowledge of the wizarding world," I joked. After all it was our shared interest in magic wands and spells that brought us together.

"Well, I didn't date you for your humour, either." Yep, he told me that right after I basically insulted his gawkiness. I didn't mean it as an insult though, and he didn't understand it as one. Just two people telling each other what they liked in the other person.

I had never been the funniest in the group, but Vic and I just made sense.

He took the bag from my hands and put it in the truck of his car. "Do you want to get a coffee or something?"

I couldn't help but grin. *Coffee heals all.* "Yeah, sounds good," I quickly replied, before he could withdraw the offer. We got in the car, and suddenly the accident seemed to belong in a totally different time. Suddenly I could relax again.

"How's your shoulder?" I was not just making conversation, I actually cared. A lot. Maybe I had just forgotten the last few days.

"It's okay," he replied, touching his right collar bone. "Still bothers me a bit when I'm playing. How's the knee? Have you been dancing?"

"Nope, not yet." I tried not to let the sadness kick in. I was sure he knew I hadn't been allowed to take classes. He also knew I would just dance about anywhere when I felt like it. "But I will again."

He smiled. "I have no doubt about it."

He started the car then. And it was like no time had passed. A song came on, and it was more than just vaguely familiar. Shakira's *Whenever, Wherever.* "Hey, Lex and I used to dance to this song at every competition for like two years!" I blurted out. Vic probably didn't care, but as soon as I heard the tunes I was back at dance.

"Isn't this song really old?" he asked. It was like one of those conversations we had a lot in the beginning. When we would tell each other stuff we didn't know about one another.

"Yeah, we were six or seven or something like that."

Maybe I could say something else. Something he probably didn't know yet. "You know I could have needed you last night." I tried to let my voice sound light, and not at all like I was accusing him of something. And I thought I actually did pretty well at that.

He thought about what to say for a moment. "I know. But I couldn't have been there for you the way you deserved." I could have understood if he had tried to get out of it. Tried to explain himself. But he didn't.

There was a time when I could tell Vic anything. No judgement. Because I knew enough secrets to blackmail him if shit got out. And the other way around. Maybe we could go back to that. Maybe we could be soulmates without being lovers. "I just needed you to be there."

He cleared his throat, eyes locked on the road. "I didn't know how to. Not with everything that had been going on. And I'm sorry."

Chapter 37

BEFORE I OPENED my eyes, I felt myself fall back into my body. Everything heavy. Everything in pain.

No! I couldn't do this again! Please don't let me do this again.

The hospital ceiling had gotten all too familiar, but this time the room was almost empty. It didn't matter though. The only person I needed was there.

"Lexi," I whispered.

She was by my side as soon as I'd said it. She'd been pacing around the room, not standing still for one second. "Hey princess."

"What happened?"

I could remember bits and pieces. Nothing solid though. I remembered breaking up with Vic, and getting into his car to get coffee. I remembered a little girl with blond hair.

"You were in another accident." She held my hand like it was the only thing she could do. But it was her presence that made all the difference.

"Is Vic okay?"

"He's fine. They have him in the other room for some tests." In her tone I could hear she thought my priorities were off. "How are *you* feeling?"

"Fine," I said before I could think about it. Then I tried moving. My legs, my arms, my head. I was still a little sore from last week's accident. But everything felt okay.

I was okay.

There was some quietness between us when Lexi examined me. My body – whether I was actually in pain – and my expression – whether I was lying.

I wasn't.

Mina had been right.

She had been right all along.

My story didn't end here, and there was so much more I still needed to do.

The silence abruptly ended when a nurse entered the room humming a song I didn't recognize. "Nadine," I said out loud, surprised.

Her warm smile greeted me. "I wish we met again under better circumstances, Jen. The good news is," She circled the bed and stood to take my vitals, "there are no visible injuries this time around."

IT WAS LEXI who took me home. She drove half the speed limit, and checked in with me every twenty seconds. She had almost freaked when the doctor tried to tell me not to get in the car with anyone under the age of 21 anymore. I neglected to tell him Vic was usually a very safe driver. I doubted he would have believed me.

Vic's parents seemed to think it was my fault we got into an accident *again.* I couldn't really blame them. All they knew was how Vic had two of them within a short period of time and both of them with me. Maybe they even knew we broke up. All the more reason to suggest it was me.

As a result, they'd refused to take me home, no matter how many times Vic said *It's not her fault.* It didn't matter that it wasn't my fault. It didn't change anything. Vic was still hurt, and I was still in pain.

I couldn't tell my parents about this. They would think it was my fault, too. They would take it to mean they had to stick around more, look out for me more, talk to me more. There hadn't been anything to talk about in years.

When we reached my house, I was almost sad there hadn't been another accident. Just to prove them wrong. Just to feel something.

And when Lexi tried to stay with me in my house, after facing one of her biggest fears for me and driving her car, I told her to leave. For her own good. Who knew what I'd do next. I didn't say the last part though. Too much.

She didn't want to hear it either way. "You almost died twice in one week! Why in hell would I ever leave you alone again?"

"I didn't die," I said quickly. *At least not this time.* And not in the literal sense anyway. *Gosh, I was seriously getting bad again!* "You need to go Lexi. I don't want you to feel like you have to stay." And I didn't want her to see me fall apart again. I didn't want to drag her down with me.

"I know I don't have to." She took a step closer, and maybe that's what made me collapse. Or maybe it was the fact that she wouldn't just leave.

"Lexi, I can't do it," I blurted out before I could change my mind. My whole life fell apart, had been falling apart, and Lexi wouldn't even leave my house. She had to know what she would get herself into. It would change her mind, but I couldn't just string her along. "I can't live like this. I have to get out. I can't keep surviving, I want to live."

She didn't react the way I had expected her to. Quite the opposite. She hugged me. Hugged me! Like I wasn't talking about being broken as hell, and not being able to commit to anything right now. Like I wasn't stuck between running away as far as possible and staying in my room until the day I died.

When she let go of me, there was a hopeful smile on her face. "Tell you what: It's your birthday in three days. Legally, you can do whatever you want after that. Survive until then, and I make sure you live forever after that."

It was sweet, but she couldn't really mean it. "You can't promise something like that."

"I can try." Lexi took both my hands in hers. Giving her words an honest feel. "And I can promise to always be there for you. I can promise to take care of you when things get bad, and to celebrate with you when things are good. I can do all of that because I care about you, and I want you in my life." It was hard to tell from the emotional state I was in myself, but there were tears in Lexi's eyes. "I know I said you don't need to be saved, but I can save you if you need me to."

Now I couldn't hold back the emotion either. I should have never doubted my best friend. "I think you already did. For the past five years there were only two, maybe three things that kept me alive."

She snorted, both of us pretending we weren't crying like babies. "Let me guess: Vic was one of them."

I didn't even have to think about it. "For a while, yes. Dance, too. And you, of course."

"Of course," she repeated, a huge grin on her face.

"Seriously, I don't know if I would have survived without you." Lexi needed to know that. Although I was almost sure she already did, I had to tell her. Now.

I pulled her into another hug. Which hopefully told her she was my person. My soulmate. The reason I was still here. The only person I needed. Wanted.

"Lexi?"

"Yeah?"

If I were a liar, I'd tell her 'I don't love you like that'. Instead I said "I love you more."

Thank You!

This book has been very hard to write, but also it has never been easier to connect to a story like I did to this one. It is a difficult topic, but it is one I have wanted to write about for a very long time. It is why I started writing.

Needless to say, I put a lot of myself in these characters and their stories. There has been a lot of hurt and worry in my life, and all I needed was someone to understand. The kid in me needed to read this book as much as current day me needed to write it. I hope this book could be this for you. And I hope you are okay.

Thank you for reading. Thank you for surviving.

Big thanks also to my friends and my sister who are there when things get bad, and to new friends who wanted to read it as soon as I mentioned my mentally unstable protagonist.

About the Author

Fiona Drechsler is a young adult writer who has published her first book 'The Girl and the Wolf: Once upon a time' in early 2023. The Once Upon A Girl-series will continue in 2024 with two more books. This is her first stand-alone novel.

Besides being an author, she is active in the theatre world. Fiona writes and directs plays, acts and dances. Like Jen, she started dancing at three years old, unlike her, Fiona's favourite style is Modern Dance.

When she is not working on her creative endeavors, Fiona enjoys traveling, coffee and petting dogs of all colours and sizes.

www.ingramcontent.com/pod-product-compliance
Lightning Source LLC
La Vergne TN
LVHW091406190726
843491LV00006B/1288
* 9 7 8 3 9 1 0 6 4 2 0 4 1 *